D1596554

The Notebooks on
Primitive Mentality

EXPLORATIONS IN INTERPRETATIVE SOCIOLOGY

GENERAL EDITORS

PHILIP RIEFF

Benjamin Franklin Professor of Sociology
University of Pennsylvania

BRYAN R. WILSON

Reader in Sociology, University of Oxford
Fellow of All Souls College

Also in this series

The Notebooks on Primitive Mentality

———◼———

Lucien Lévy-Bruhl

with a Preface by Maurice Leenhardt

Translated by Peter Rivière

Harper & Row Publishers
New York, Evanston, San Francisco

LIBRARY OF CONGRESS CATALOG CARD NUMBER: 74–33110

STANDARD BOOK NUMBER: 0–06–136174–7

First published in French in 1949 as *Carnets*
and translated by arrangement with Presses
Universitaires de France.

PRINTED IN GREAT BRITAIN

Translator's acknowledgements

I wish to record my thanks and debt to Sarah Rivière
and Rodney Needham both of whom gave me vital
and invaluable assistance in the preparation of this
translation.

P.G.R.

114 054
104054

Contents

Preface

by Maurice Leenhardt

Thin, cheap notebooks in black oilcloth and with thirty small
pages of poor cross-ruled paper. The philosopher had the habit
of keeping one in his pocket, and when, out walking, an idea in
connection with his thoughts came to him he used to sit and write
it down. The notebooks which have been recovered relate to the
last months of his life. Their pages are filled with a fine, regular
hand, without corrections. The conclusion is always at the foot
of the page as if the space of the wording had been measured
in advance. The place and the date appear underneath, so that
it is possible to follow Lévy-Bruhl on his outings in the Bois
de Boulogne, at Bagatelle, and on the coasts of Normandy and
Brittany. On the inner side of the cover he put his name and
address and . . . a list of contents. Because he used to reread his
notes and discuss them with himself, the real title which should
be given to this collection could well be: *The Soliloquies of Lévy-
Bruhl.*

In the upheavals of the war years, his books and documents
had disappeared, but owing to the filial piety of his children, his
elder son found and saved these last notebooks. They are as
precious as a key which opens the last doors to a treasure house.

The simple appearance of these notebooks and the richness of
their content might appear as a very modest symbol of the
philosopher's personality. Tall and thin, nothing distinguished
him from the crowd except for a look that was both assured and
searching, with his head slightly inclined, always in a listening
position. Singleness of mind, breadth of knowledge, accuracy,
ability, caution, and impartiality, all those qualities which confer
intellectual authority he had and used with tact. There was a
perfect balance between the humanity of his person and that of
his thought. The former was thoughtful, the latter remained
human.

These characteristics are in equal evidence throughout the

whole length of his life. As early as the École Normale, the young
student looks at the world with an interest tinged with sympathy.
He believes in modern man, formed by a secular culture and
respecting all the values which give him dignity. At that period
a Kantian, and for some time after, he was not afraid to choose
'Responsibility' as a thesis subject. He took his place in the fine
company of his time, Lanson, Salomon Reinach, Émile Bourgeois,
Baudrillart, Bergson, Paul Desjardins, and Jaurès as his friends.
The friendship which bound him to the last and the support
which he gave him led him, after the murder of Jaurès, to write,
in a few pages, the most illuminating biography possible, encap-
sulating the light and flavour of an intelligent and altruistic life;
certainly the best pages on the great democratic leader. The
manner of this little book reveals Lévy-Bruhl's very personality:
burning convictions, discretion out of respect for another, regard
for the truth, modesty, a collection of qualities which explain the
elegant moderation of his style, and the combination of a wise,
well-balanced and tolerant mind with the daring of a constantly
active thought.

When very young, Boutmy gave him the job of teaching the
history of political thought and public opinion in Germany and
England at the École des Sciences Politiques which had just been
founded, and he published, as a consequence of his lectures, his
brilliant book *L'Allemagne depuis Leibniz*. Before long he had a
lecturership at the École Normale, and then succeeded Boutroux
at the Sorbonne in the Chair of the History of Philosophy.

Was it his preference for problems concerning man and his
knowledge of German thought which led him, with Jacobi, to the
study of the philosophies of sensation?

However, he was disappointed in them. He held that they
refute themselves 'in depriving reason of the supreme function of
judging between true and false', and contribute to the mainten-
ance of morals of belief and feeling. Could it be that their
influence profits from the diverging paths of science and metaphysics? A growing agnosticism leaves in suspense questions that
are too important for man to consent to leave unanswered. And
he wondered if this agnosticism might not be 'less a solution in
itself than the sign of a transference'?

In any case Lévy-Bruhl wanted to know about it. He turned

back to Comte and published a lucid book on him. The influence of positivism was to make him lose the taste, he said, 'for all philosophy which is not strictly bound to the history of science and to the current state of scientific research and speculation'. Before long Durkheim drew him to sociology. He had too much a mind of his own to submit to the authority of a master, but he occupied himself in sociology energetically, and embodied his new investigations in his famous work *Ethics and Moral Science*. —'To one entirely definite social state corresponds one system (more or less harmonious) of entirely definite moral rules, and one alone.'—The success was resounding. Lévy-Bruhl was forty-six years old. It could be believed that he had found his way and was going simply to press on further. But the debates surrounding his book, the attention he paid to objections and his insatiable eagerness for research made him judge his works to be too theoretical. He had to keep closer to the facts about mankind.

After all, he asked himself, is it certain that the human mind is everywhere the same? Is it right, without checking, to be reconciled to the consensus of philosophers, indeed to that of the English school of anthropology? And in order to widen his knowledge of the human mind, he would attempt the study of this mind in the midst of the society furthest from our own. The differences, if they exist, will then appear in their greatest contrast.

And from here starts his brilliant advance into the anthropological domain.

But once it is a matter of formulating his thought in the midst of the innumerable and new data which he discovers, a difficulty arises: the differences from our mental habits are so great that no existing vocabulary can express them. It is necessary for Lévy-Bruhl to create an adequate language. For a time he succeeds in doing so. But at what a price! As early as his first volume, *How Natives Think*, he coins the expressions: prelogical, law of participation, mystical. Immediately he is attacked on the first two formulae, and on all that they might mean.

In the face of these attacks, Lévy-Bruhl, not out of regard for the public, but on his own account—for he adopted any objection he thought reasonable—tones down what offends, consolidates and makes clear what is not understood. The five volumes which are to follow will be attempts to explain the facts of the first better, whether it be causality in the volume *Primitive Mentality*, or participation and the affective category in *Le Surnaturel et la Nature (Primitives and the Supernatural)*, *L'Âme primitive (The 'Soul' of the Primitive)*, *La Mythologie primitive*, and *L' Expérience mystique et les symboles chez primitifs*.

His books are translated. He has every satisfaction which a thinker can have—save that satisfaction of completely agreeing with himself.

It is here that the notebooks saved from the ravages of war acquire their full interest.

Without them we would not know about the high-minded concern in the thought of the philosopher whose external appearance gave the impression of serenity.

What was the object of this concern? Participation. Between the first volume—*How Natives Think* (1910)—and the sixth—*L'Expérience mystique* (1937)—there is a great gap. In the first he asserts, in the last he qualifies endlessly. A final work in which Lévy-Bruhl would have given the definitive conclusion is missing. Perhaps the rediscovered notebooks may allow us to guess what this last book might have contained? From the activity of his thought in the course of his walks, no one can say that Lévy-Bruhl had stopped at those last conclusions. These notebooks are like the reminder of an awakening. Private notes, similar to the rough sketches made with curved and redrawn lines which the artist does not exhibit; the philosopher would never have sent them for publication just as they are, with their repetitions and reiterations.

They show the deepening of his thought. Lévy-Bruhl, without abandoning anything which is essential to him, reduces in importance what is not indispensable; he rejects the term 'prelogical' as definitely wrong; he gives up presenting participation in the form of a law, which could lead to confusion. 'The general scheme of representation and of knowledge cannot be suitable for taking account of participation. This last does not result from cognitive mental activity.'

With his admirable serenity, the philosopher scrutinizes and modifies his previous conclusions when they cease to be compatible with the greater part of the truth which he has been able to discern. As a logician of the nineteenth century, he is attentive to everything which can enlighten him; he observes what the twentieth century brings. It is the reading of an article by Einstein that reveals to him a suggestive and new aspect of reality.

The physicist has simply stated that what is incomprehensible in the world is precisely that it can be understood. Lévy-Bruhl's thought responds marvellously to this statement. At once, it takes up the point: 'The intelligibility of the sensible world, ordered and ruled by science, is for ever unintelligible. It is a fact which is forced upon us . . . It is thus not an absolute.'

He jumps at the escape opened up by this suppression of the absolute: primitive man takes the mythical world as real and that is unintelligible. Now if the unintelligibility of the rational world is itself intelligible, might there not be in this attitude of primitive man a sort of difference in degree only and 'a sort of transference of the unintelligibility in detail onto the world given in its totality'?

A transference. This psychological term had already arisen when he was studying the philosophies of sensation. It justifies a change of plan. It is like an incitement to Lévy-Bruhl to take up his dialectic again without the intense concern for traditional logic.

When he rereads various reports,[1] it becomes much clearer to him that concepts, representations, and ideas may be not ordered and classified but merely juxtaposed. On this point it is to be regretted that he did not resort in his dialectical endeavour to everything which aesthetics offers for the elucidation of the problem! As a canoe prow, for example, fashioned after the head of a crocodile, with the representation of feathers and human face—a saurian relation of the feathered serpent represents for every native the idea of his ancestor who was lizard, man and bird. This matter, incomprehensible in speech because of the contradictions and incompatibilities which it contains, becomes clear when, instead of being spoken, it is translated into a form. Juxtapositions which logic does not comprehend when they are presented in speech, here seem well ordered in the work of art. The remarks of the artist praising his multiform ancestor appear

---

[1] Leenhardt's manuscript to which he alludes is that of the article 'Religion des primitifs actuels' destined for *L'histoire des Religions* (Quillet's edited collection) and, because of the war, not published until 1946.

incoherent; art, on the contrary, reveals the coherence of his thought, and that of his brothers who read in his sculpture exactly what he wanted to express. In this work there is balance, classification, distinction of motifs, order, and finally logic. What is the gap between the distinctions which have governed the choice, guided the artist's hand, and what will before long be called a concept?

It is aesthetics which puts a first coherence in primitive man's mind. Lévy-Bruhl did not look in this direction, whence his subtlety might have derived the richest explanations.

In fact there are two domains which, at the end of the last century, were still closed and which his work has helped to open; that of the aesthetics of primitive man, and that of myth.

Of the former, he did little more than cross the threshold. He loved to show the objects of native art which he might have in his hall or in his desk, and his philosopher friends had trouble in sharing his enthusiasm. Although he did not avowedly make use of the intuition which he had about the value of these objects for the understanding of the human mind, the interest which he showed in this art helped to confer upon it the importance which it has since acquired in the mind of everyone.

Of the second domain, myth, he has, on the contrary, crossed the threshold, and has mapped out a way where all mythologists come to join him. The study of primitive mentality was to lead him to reconsider the age-old discredit in which mythologies were held. He was not the first to indicate the value of myths, but he was the first to push so far their study in primitive tradition. He had a presentiment of their importance even as early as his first work, *How Natives Think*, when he posed the suggestive question 'Might myths thus be products of the primitive mentality which appear when it is endeavouring to realize a participation which is not felt directly?' But, at the time, so strong was the Aristotelian discipline that when he came later to write *La Mythologie primitive* he did not go beyond the intuition which he had had when asking this question twenty years earlier, before the First World War. He concedes to myth the value of a relaxation of our mind which is always in tension, a relaxation which is moreover necessary to suspend the constraint on it, to free its repressed tendencies, and to discover a freedom of thought in the experience of reality. But this relaxation is the property of recreation, and yet it seems that this recreation is only, in Lévy-Bruhl's eyes, a concession to our rational weakness. To go beyond this conclusion had appeared to him as definitely unwise. This point can be argued with reference to those narratives that he classed under the rubric of stories. He finds there good examples of the fluidity of thought in primitive men. But must it be forgotten that they are still, in the eyes of primitive men, myths, the living revealers of reality? Like that of the Guinean whose skin is covered in ulcers. From time to time he lays it aside in order to put on wings and fly. A young girl catches him at his trick and while he is flying she throws his nasty skin in the fire. When he lands and looks for his skin in order to put it on again, he receives the attentions of the young girl. This whole story indicates the stages through which the unfortunate man passes, now ulcerous, now full of hope and winged, victorious at last and passing thrilling hours of passionate excitement. Primitive men do not have abstract terms in order to relate the psychology of love. They define the event by such accounts as this, and it is in the course of its details that the Papuans obtain knowledge of its nature.

It is agreed now that myth is a form of knowledge, but at the time Lévy-Bruhl, with reservation, might not have contradicted this, also he would not have been able to agree.[1] This would have been to ask him to make a leap into the unknown, and his notebooks reveal the care with which he advanced along the paths which he was opening up. To understand this reverse, it is necessary to take into account the great advance with regard to primitive men and anthropology made by Lévy-Bruhl over his contemporaries. If the rigidity of logic's framework always supports the mind and guides its flashes of brilliancy, the inflexibility of our categories has also become an obstacle to it. We can thus appreciate Lévy-Bruhl's merit in his effort to penetrate yet further into the primitive mentality, in search of forgotten categories.

Lévy-Bruhl, as a philosopher, was certainly not heartened by those who doubted his conclusions because he had not been in

---

[1] It is this which determined the choice of our lectures 'Formes mythiques de la vie des Mélanésiens' in the Conférences Loubat at the Collège du France in 1942, and published in 1947 under the title *Do Kamo (La personne et le mythe dans le monde mélanésien)*.

B

the field. But this failing due to old age indicates the special aptitude which he had for ceaselessly cross-checking the narratives from books and the stories of missionaries and travellers whom he questioned with shrewdness and tact. He did not describe the native, and it would even be possible to say that the primitive man of whom he speaks does not really exist. But in the course of his work he has disengaged a type of mentality, of such a sort that white men and black men, civilized men and precivilized men, have always recognized in it some features of their own mind. This successful effort allowed him to go beyond the logic which he employed with so strict a discipline in order to show that in the mind functions assert themselves which even the bonds of logic cannot constrain.

Is it not this same reason, the novelty of his work at the time, which explains the choice of the term 'mystical' in his vocabulary, despite its inadequacy and despite even that it was not acceptable to him? If it should be suggested to him that the term 'mystical' be withdrawn and 'mythical' used instead, he opposed it with his gentle smile. He understood by this word 'imperceptible and yet real forces'. As if this designation of force were not itself 'a word binding an event to a given moment', that is to say a myth already. As if a force were not the revelation of an order of realities not yet fully understood and which dictates commensurate behaviour. And might not this order itself proceed from the human mind in forms and resonances the order of which we still do not well understand?

In reality, 'mystical' was and still is the term of escape which covers everything in human behaviour that defies clear analysis. It has become well established today, although anthropologists have abandoned it save only for deliberate use when it is a question of mysticism or of absorption in the divinity. In fact, Lévy-Bruhl, in creating a language suitable for his work in the domain of primitive men, was in the situation of the pioneer who introduces a plant into a new climate. He cannot know whether, once acclimatized, it will not spread like a weed. This is rather like what happened to the term 'mystical'.

Lévy-Bruhl used the term in order to designate the affective fringe which borders all human experience and may even monopolize it. He divided all human experience into ordinary experience and mystical experience. But at the lowest level of thought where the latter is met the sense of the mystical is as though dissolved; it leaves around the experience a fuzziness similar to the halation round a badly developed negative. The truth of the matter, in his opinion, is that primitive man does not make use of the concept as we do. Not caring about secondary causes, he retains only the primary cause. Because of this lack in the notion of causality the mystical experience remains at the level of ordinary experience, and the emotion which it arouses prevents the mind from understanding the phenomenon objectively. The epithet 'mystical' is not appropriate where affectivity smothers rationality and common sense. The term 'mythical', and sometimes 'magical', would often be more suitable. But whereas Lévy-Bruhl courageously abandoned the unsatisfactory term 'prelogical' and thus freed participation from a contradictory aspect with which he had harnessed it, his attachment to the term 'mystical' in human experience has prevented him on the contrary from changing it, and, as a result, from answering more clearly the question quoted above which he had asked himself at the end of *How Natives Think*, on the connections between participation and myth.

Thus participation will remain inherent in mystical experience as it was already in its capacity as the affective category of the supernatural. It is this which makes the task so difficult for the philosopher who had at first thought to make it fit into the framework of our categories.

Those parts of these notebooks which show Lévy-Bruhl in search of the true nature of participation make moving reading. With admirable conformity to the rules of logical thought, he again takes the facts one after another, studies them, seeks an order in them, turns them round and round, digs into them, weighs them, retains or rejects them—it might be said as a chemist among his retorts, the thinker is followed through the laboratory of his thought.

Lévy-Bruhl wished to demonstrate, through the universality of some primitive aspects of mentality, the unity of the human mind in space and time. From the fact of belonging to an archaic or a modern culture, the mind may have a different orientation, but it stays the same; and always, to varying degrees, in its every resource, participation is at work.

If the latter seems to us irreconcilable with the norms of our intelligence, is this not because we take it for granted that things are given in the first place, and that afterwards they participate in some force or other without it being understood how?

It is fallacious, however, to take this order for granted. 'In order that things shall be given and that they shall exist, participations are already necessary. Participation is not a fusion of things which lose or conserve their identity at one and the same time; it enters into their very constitution. Without it they would not be given and would have no existence. It is immanent in the individual, a condition of existence. To exist is to participate in a mystical force, essence, and reality.'

It is not a question of slipping into a sort of ontology. Lévy-Bruhl, from the beginning of his inquiry, at the period when he explained participation with the help of the prelogical, had already seen that the understanding of this participation would open up some unexpected paths. He finished his book *How Natives Think* with this sentence:

'If it is true that our mental activity is logical and prelogical at one and the same time, the history of religious dogmas and of philosophical systems may henceforth be explained in a new light.'

Twenty-eight years later, in the middle of the difficult years of war, post-war and pre-war, he cast off everything which might hinder his thought. Participation has its place in the human mind. But still he knows nothing about the nature of participation. A sharply painful ignorance:

'But where begins and where ends the field of participation? Why has it needed twenty centuries to ascertain its functioning? Why have not Plato, Malebranche, and the metaphysicians who have spoken of it, not attributed to it its function in the mind?'

But from the knowledge he has acquired, he concludes:

'Participation is not accounted for, it cannot be explained, it ought not to be, it has no need of legitimation, yet one sees its necessary place in the human mind—and as a consequence its role in religion, metaphysics, art, and even in the conception of the entirety of nature.'

Philosophers, anthropologists, biologists, psychologists and psychiatrists continue to scutinize what they uncover about man. Participation remains a still more unfathomable field. One goes so far as to ask if it is not in itself that the conceptual distinction lies? And many other questions ranging from logic to meta-physics. But at the base of all these labours, Lévy-Bruhl's thought retains its initial value. A vivid dialectic is not a self-sufficient argument; it is an arrangement of facts which reveals aspects of the human mind. It puts the problems in concrete form, and it invites their re-examination.

Having reached this level, scaled with such difficulty, where participation has at last found its function and place in the human mind, Lévy-Bruhl had the right to pause a while. The laws of participation henceforth being established, he allows his thought to explore the surrounds of this conclusion. Very objec-tively he considers the weak points that still exist, the unexplored regions that remain and whence can arise some unexpected facts. In the final lines of his last notebook, he notes the necessity for a sociological study of participation: he insists on new research into myth.

Marcel Mauss, late in the day, also took an interest in myth. It is a very revealing thing to see these two thinkers, both char-acteristic of the end of the nineteenth century, finally meeting in a similar preoccupation, which is to be that of the twentieth century. The enthusiasm for myth among primitive men had made Mauss doubt that myth was simply the prologue to rites. And Lévy-Bruhl, less concerned with morphology, had in his turn doubted that religion was solely myth.

In his *Mythologie primitive*,[1] Lévy-Bruhl had posed a cautious question, like the noting down of an intuition, and had asked whether there might not exist, among primitive peoples, a pre-religion. In reading this it is to be seen that he disagrees with Durkheim, for whom religion has but a given and constant con-tent, through which the religious phenomenon endures with the same features, comprising nothing outmoded, and in which the old questions are still the present ones. The 'Elementary Forms', by the title of his book, pertain to a type of phenomenon evolving according to a determinate series. They proceed from a substan-tialist idea according to which religion appears static. Lévy-Bruhl, on the contrary, is struck by the gulf which exists between organized and primitive religions, which precede any attempt at organization. Whence comes the prefix 'pre' by which he

[3] p. 218.

qualifies them. Already and entirely they form part of social
life, and they comprise a dynamism which animates the whole.
Historians of religion will draw their inspiration from Lévy-
Bruhl's intuition to separate the enthusiasm of primitive life filled
with wholly magical exchange and communion from the *opus
operatum* of religions classed as advanced. Perhaps they will
judge the collective fervour and loyalty of primitive men parallel,
on the sociological level only, to that which is spiritually required
in every religion that has as a principle piety 'in thought and in
truth'. The one is only social, the other is personal. But the
boundaries between the two are precisely one of the objectives
of the sociology of religion. Lévy-Bruhl did not seek to draw out
the full significance of this intuition whose richness I once
praised to his face. But it is linked to the whole problem of participation.

It also answers, and in another way, an attempt which has
been made to class Lévy-Bruhl as a metaphysician. It even happened that one day an author presented him with the manuscript
of a work on this theme. Lévy-Bruhl read it, annotated it now
and then, but declined to accept the thesis and begged the author
'not to conceal their disagreement'. This happened a few days
before his death, and that date seals with solemnity this refusal.

The whole time his thinking needed to rest on a concrete fact
or a precise datum. Thence came that thoroughgoing examination which was the object of his research: not just the individual
himself, the abstract being, capable of slipping away and taking
the form of a god, but rather the individual of our daily experience, who, at the antipodes just as here, lives through ex-
changes, and whose mind is diversely modelled by the effects of
their circulation. This is a sociological aspect of the individual.

Whether it is a matter of the individual or religion, Lévy-
Bruhl masters his research by not neglecting any morphological
or human aspect of his subject-matter, and he operates with a
soundness of method a little after the manner of a phenomenolo-
gist. But his intuition is to remain on the sociological plane. In
this way he has prepared the materials and he has laid the first
foundations of a sociology of knowledge. To make him overstep
this limit, however, in order to include him in the constellation of
metaphysicians, will always indicate an excess of zeal, confusion,
and, finally, a betrayal of his thought.

As a philosopher, he masters the disciplines but belongs to none. And with regard to man, he frees them all. After Lévy-Bruhl, one no longer speaks of man as one did before. Psychologists, psychiatrists, psychoanalysts, etc., have drawn from his observations suggestions and material for comparison. And anthropology, from the fact of the universality in human mentality of characteristics called primitive, has at last been able to cross the too narrow limits which have been assigned to it. Across the most varied races, the mind of man is one in its diversity. It is the study of these diversities and these races which remains its greatest task.

Thus Lévy-Bruhl's work closes the nineteenth century at the same moment as it inaugurates the twentieth century, eager for a wider view of the condition of man.

But these notebooks, published posthumously almost in the middle of the twentieth century, provide something more.

They indicate his true position and reveal his proper role with regard to all that marginal fringe of the human mind which seemed to escape what were called the laws of the mind.

They also explain through the fact of participation the interaction between the social group and individuality. A whole dark side of the life of human societies has been illuminated. Henceforth it is not possible to equate primitive with elementary according to the confusion created by Durkheim. There is no necessary continuity. Evolutionism and human progress form a superannuated tautology.

They reveal above all the extraordinary unity of Lévy-Bruhl's life.

Throughout its length, there is the same intellectual probity in the course of a struggle which starts when the young professor interests himself in the philosophies of sensation, acquires new strength from positivism, and before long, without any illusions about the weakness of the human mind, notes one day: 'Metaphysical ethics, ethics found *a priori*, no longer exists. Scientific ethics does not yet exist, if it is ever to exist ... In this interregnum, the position is held by the ethics of belief and sensation.' Can one not discern here, cast ahead, the Ariadnean thread of his research? The link that will unite his book *How Natives Think* to *Ethics and Moral Science* of eight years before? And the link that twenty-eight years later will unite to *How Natives*

Think the pages of these notebooks, summarized from the beginning in the affirmation: 'To be is to participate.'

It is no longer the analysis of moral science or primitive mentality that he attempts; what he has isolated is a structural element of man. He leaves the formula so that others after him may separate out the great riches which it contains for the understanding of the human mind.

Note

In this volume, Lévy-Bruhl's numerical references to his earlier works are as follows:

Volume I.   *How Natives Think.*
Volume II.   *Primitive Mentality.*
Volume III. *The 'Soul' of the Primitive.*
Volume IV.   *Primitives and the Supernatural.*
Volume V.   *La Mythologie primitive.*
Volume VI.   *L'Expérience mystique et les symboles chez les primitifs.*

Notebook I
January–May 1938

The starting point for a rather deeper study of participation seems to me to be the fact that our way of formulating it, or even simply expressing it in our vocabulary with our concepts, falsifies it, and moreover gives it an unintelligible appearance which it does not necessarily have.

In the main, this happens because we connect it, in whole or in part, with mental activity in so far as this is representational or cognitive; and because, in doing this, we inevitably apply to it the general scheme of representation and knowledge as established by ancient philosophy, and by modern psychological thought or attempts at a theory of knowledge. Now, to try to apply this scheme to participation is to do it violence and to distort it. This is the feeling I had when I qualified the category of the supernatural, where participation is concerned, as affective, and when I insisted repeatedly on the impossibility of clearly analysing participations and of making them comprehensible to the intelligence. But these general remarks provide no positive contribution to the illumination of participation's true nature. It is necessary to return to the direct study of the facts.

Let us take some example of undeniable participation, and let us try to see how our way of expressing it misrepresents it or at least deforms it. Take the participation between the deceased who has become a *sovai*-ghost of the Orokaiva—and the corpse which lies in the hut. It is equally true to say that the corpse is the deceased, and that it is not; this proves that neither expression is correct. We are obliged to say rather that there is participation between the ghost and the corpse, such that the action exercised on the corpse reacts directly on the ghost, so that the latter is fed and its thirst slaked when the corpse is given food and drink, so that it suffers from the cold when the corpse is exposed, etc. The question is: is there a difference between the participation thus expressed in our language and what really exists in the consciousness of primitive man, and if so, what is it?

There is at least one difference, as is evident from the following consideration. For us the participation between the ghost and the corpse presupposes that primitive man represents to himself separately the ghost and the corpse and feels that these two representations are not independent of one another, do not exist separately; that is to say the ghost and the corpse constitute together a duality-unity, in short they participate in one another.

Now this description, about which there is nothing that makes us suspect that it may not be right—because we have clearly distinct representations of the deceased and his corpse and because the participation between them (which we do not feel but which, through instinctive fellow feeling, we accept as felt by primitive men) seems to us to be necessarily posterior to these representations—does not faithfully reproduce what goes on in primitive men.

In the first place, neither the ghost nor the corpse is for primitive men what it is for us (easy to show from the facts: the corpse does not speak, but it hears, etc.).

Then—and here is the most important point—participation is not established between the more or less clearly represented deceased and corpse (in which case it would be of the nature of a relationship or connection, and it should be possible to make it easily comprehensible); it does not come after these representations, it does not presuppose them: it is before them, or at least simultaneous with them. What is given *in the first place* is participation.

But, it will be said, this way of presenting things is unreasonable and untenable. Participation between what? How can there be participation if the primitive man does not represent to himself the beings or objects which participate with one another? Is it not evident, that, on the contrary, he has a very vivid and moving representation of the ghost and the corpse?—Agreed. But he has them only so far as they are implicit in the participation, he does not make them explicit as we do. We picture the ghost and the corpse, and from that, for the primitive man, arises between them an intimate participation which forms a duality-unity. For the primitive man it is this duality-unity which is—not thought—

but felt first, and it is then, if he reflects, that he recognizes a participation between the ghost on the one hand, and the corpse on the other. There is developed in him a complex comprised of what we call affective elements and representative elements (the latter moreover the more subordinate to the former as his emotion is more violent and deeper). When, in order to express this complex, we say that primitive man feels an intimate participation between the ghost and the corpse, this expression is right in so far as we say: he *feels*. But it ceases to be right when we say that he feels it between two given terms or things. It is from our point of view that they are given first, and participation is established between them and felt afterwards. From the point of view of primitive man's consciousness what is given is the complex, that is to say above all emotion caused by the death, the felt participation; the isolated representation of either the corpse or the ghost, if it comes, comes only afterwards. We have great difficulty in accepting and still more in understanding this because we always use concepts and because the concept of participation seems to us necessarily to involve the presence of those concepts of the things between which the participation is established, even if it is only felt. But the study which we are attempting is only possible if we always guard against endowing primitive men with our mental habits. Now without doubt they are not incapable of forming concepts, and indeed they do form them. But in the circumstance in question the predominance of affective elements is such that participation is essentially feeling and is realized without previous concepts.

January 20th, 1938.

INDEPENDENT OF LOGICAL AND PHYSICAL CONDITIONS

In other words, the duality-unity of ghost-corpse, which we term thus because of the intimate participation which ensures that the two are felt at one and the same time as distinct and yet forming only one being, is felt as a fact where the two beings which participate with one another form only one. This seems surprising to us. But it is a question of the nature of the deceased whose unity, while alive, was naturally felt as incontestable. Death disunites this individual and separates the ghost from the corpse.

For us this separation is total and final. In spite of the piety which is attached to the remains of the loved ones who have been lost, we consider that memory alone unites the 'mortal remains' and the individual who, at least for the mass of believers, survives indestructible.

For primitive man it is completely different. First, he has no clear idea, or even no idea at all, of matter (body, corpse) and soul (spirit, immaterial reality), and, accordingly, in so far as he represents a principle of life, a soul, it is at one and the same time spiritual and material; as a matter of fact it is neither one nor the other in the sense that we understand them (following Elsdon Best), and it is necessary to say as much for the body or corpse, bone or skull which is never for primitive man the entirely inanimate object which it is for us. Then, it is true that for primitive man as for us death breaks the unity of the individual: the ghost withdraws, and while remaining in the neighbourhood, it is henceforth separated from the corpse. But here is where lies an essential difference between the primitive mentality and ours.

For primitive men the fact that the ghost and the corpse are located in parts of space separate from each other does not prevent them from still constituting a duality-unity. Despite the fact that a kilometre or two separates them, the corpse and the ghost are always felt as one individual, whose duality and separateness (here the corpse, there the ghost) do not prevent it from being felt as one. Here is the essence of participation, of which one of the characteristics is that the bi-presence is not an obstacle to what may be felt. For us, on the contrary, there is here an invincible block. We are indeed forced to accept that primitive man feels between the ghost and the corpse a participation that forms for him a duality-unity of which, *first and foremost*, he feels the unity, but we do not manage to understand how he is able to represent things to himself in this way.

Indeed, it is not understandable. But even that ought to enlighten us and show us that in using the words 'understand' and 'represent' here we are taking a wrong turn and entering a cul-de-sac. The participation that makes of the ghost—here—and the corpse—there—one and the same reality, a duality-unity, is neither thought nor represented, and accordingly it is not a thing of the intellect. The complex in which it is enveloped, in the consciousness of primitive man, is essentially affective. In so

far as it is affective—which it eminently is—participation has
nothing to do with the logical or physical conditions of possibility.
The corpse is here in the hut where the man died. The ghost
wanders in the neighbourhood, or sets out for the land of the
dead. The primitive man is not unaware of this, he knows that
a distance separates them. From the point of view of thought, if
it were possible to make him see it like this, he would recognize,
like us, that there are two distinct realities. But from the affective
point of view which predominates in the complex where participation is included, duality-unity has no need of being possible:
it is felt, therefore it is real; objectively real.

January 20th, 1938.

COMPARISON WITH GRUBB'S CASE

There is, therefore, for the primitive mentality an objectivity
which is independent of the conditions of possibility, and this is
revealed in participation. We have just seen it in the case of
participation between ghost and corpse. Another, very different
example will help us form an idea of this objectivity and of this
participation. Grubb's example is not a case of participation, but
simply of reality independent of the conditions of possibility.
But that makes it only that more interesting to compare with a
case of participation and to examine what they have in common.

Grubb argues with the Indian who asks him for an indemnity
for the pumpkins stolen by him from his garden. Grubb explains
to the Indian that he cannot have committed this theft since at
the time indicated by the Indian he was 150 miles away. The
Indian acknowledges this. The alibi thus seems decisive and the
affair settled. Not at all, the Indians persists in his claim. Very
surprised, Grubb has the ability to recognize that he has found
himself in the presence of something quite interesting. He realizes
that it is in a dream that the Indian saw him enter the garden,
take the pumpkins, and leave with them. For the Indian what
he has thus seen in a dream is real, and he has no reason to doubt
it. At that moment, Grubb did indeed enter the garden and did
indeed commit there the theft which the Lengua witnessed.
Grubb does not argue against the fact of the dream. It is enough
for him to point out to the Indian that on the day in question, he

was 150 miles away—, therefore it was impossible for him to have been in the Indian's village.

What Grubb did not see is that for the Indian this impossibility—which provides the conclusive force of the alibi—does not exist. Grubb is 150 miles away. The Indian accepts this. But he also admits as no less true that on the same day he entered the garden of his village. How can he allow the two simultaneous presences of Grubb in two places 150 miles apart? This is what Grubb finds unintelligible in an Indian who is not a fool and who reasons normally.—But the Indian in vain reasons normally with Grubb: there is between them this difference, which Grubb does not suspect, that in Grubb's view something impossible is certainly not real, whereas in the Indian's eyes something felt as real is definitely real, whether it is possible or not. What the dream reveals is true: nothing can prevail against this certainty. If you make him see that this reality is incompatible with another no less certain reality, and if he understands what his interlocutor is getting at he will be for a longer or shorter time nonplussed, perplexed, perhaps abashed, but he will not abandon his assertion. He will put up with two incompatible certainties, and unlike the white man will not believe himself obliged to choose.

No more does the primitive man choose when he feels that the deceased is at one and the same time the ghost who wanders in the neighbourhood, and the immobile corpse on the bed. Know as he might that they make two; the participation between the ghost and the corpse forms a duality-unity which has no need to be intelligible in order to be real. Likewise the Grubb who is seen in the garden by the Indian (in his dream) and the Grubb who is effectively 150 miles from there are two Grubbs, and at the same time they are one and the same person because Grubb is held responsible for what he did in the garden when the Indian saw him there. It is not only a marvellous example of bi-presence: it is also a limit case of duality-unity. There are two Grubbs at the same moment in two different places and, at the same time, there is for both of them only a single Grubb. The Lengua sees no difficulty here even when it is shown to him that this cannot be. The comparison of this case with participation is *illuminating*.

January 21st, 1938.

CONTRADICTION (LOGICAL) AND INCOMPATIBILITY

In trying to define better the characteristic of the primitive mentality from the logical point of view, that is to say in what way precisely it differs from ours from this point of view, I understand why the word prelogical has given rise to so many objections, in part justified—and that my ideas were not sufficiently matured and elucidated. I have not been sufficiently careful when speaking of 'contradiction'. In the strict sense, many things and propositions which primitive men allow and which we reject as absurd are not properly speaking contradictions: they are unacceptable to our mind, and the primitive mentality accepts them. But is it necessary to explain this undeniable fact by saying that those minds do not have the same logical demands as ours? I have often said so without close examination as to whether this opinion does not go beyond what the facts allow to be asserted.

Take, for example, the Grubb case. The missionary calls attention to the fact that if he were 100 miles away from the Indian's village he could not, that same day, enter the latter's garden. The conclusion compels recognition. The Indian, who had not thought of this, is confused at first; but straightaway he recovers himself and maintains his statement. He recognizes that Grubb was far away on that day, but none the less persists in believing that he has seen him in his garden.

Does it follow that the logical requirements of his mind are weaker than those of ours and that his accommodates an obvious contradiction?—It is true to say that the two propositions which he admits at the same time: Grubb is in place B.—Grubb, the same day, is at place A, 100 miles away, are incompatible. We do not see how the second can be true if the first is, and the other way round. But incompatible is not contradictory. The incompatibility of the propositions constitutes a *physical* impossibility, but not a logical impossibility. Bi-presence and the multi-presence seem to us inadmissable; nevertheless the omnipresence of God, in the thought of the great majority of believers, is a local presence which is simultaneously real in an infinity of places. Lots of primitive peoples—the Bantu for example—accept without difficulty the bi-presence and even the multi-presence of their dead and many white peoples do the same. If one shows them the

C

problem, they will recognize it, they will acknowledge even the incompatibility of the propositions (as do also the Lengua) but they will not find themselves convinced of absurdity as if one had proved to them that the propositions are logically contradictory.

If therefore I do not wish to go beyond what the facts permit to be affirmed, I will just say: the primitive mentality allows, without being shaken, some incompatibilities which ours rejects instinctively (give a certain number of facts).

The question will then arise: what is the logical significance of these incompatibilities? Are they all similar, or is there need to distinguish many sorts? We immediately see that the contradictory propositions are incompatible. But primitive men never formulate it thus, and barely work with concepts. Their incompatible propositions express facts which do not seem to us to be possibly real at the same time. Therefore it is a matter, as I have just written, of a physical impossibility. What it is necessary to examine now is if, in the final analysis, it does not involve a logical impossibility, and what exactly incompatibility means.

Bagatelle: March 3rd, 1938.

I have already had occasion to speak of incompatibilities which the primitive mentality does not seem to notice, and which arrest our attention: in particular the facts of bi-presence and duality-unities. There will be reason to return to these and examine them more closely in order to see if there are questions of a truly logical order involved. We will see this later.

But there are other incompatibilities which we reject straight off and before which the unbiased primitive mentality experiences no confusion. Of what really consists the difference in attitudes in these cases? Can we reduce it to less exacting logical requirements?

Take the case of the Trumai. According to the Bororo, the Trumai pass the night at the bottom of the river. Impossible, says K. von den Steinen: men cannot sleep at the bottom of the water. They are not fish. This reasoning does not convince the Bororo at all. It seems to us irrefutable. The Trumai are men. Men submerged for some minutes are asphyxiated and die. Therefore either the Trumai are men and so it is untrue that they pass the nights in the water—or, if the fact is right, they are not men. It is necessary to choose. Now there is no doubt that they are men. Therefore they do not survive in the water. It is a necessary consequence. If the Bororo do not grasp this, and if, when it is put before their eyes, they still remain unconvinced, must it not be concluded that their mind does not have the same logical exigencies as ours?

A conclusion that seems to impose itself, and yet prematurely. It presupposes that in the mind of the Bororo there exists the same representation of the natural order in all ways similar to that in ours; that, for example, the things of nature have there a fixed and stable definition, and that, for example, if one allows at one and the same time this definition and something which is excluded by it one contradicts oneself. The nature of the human being is such that he cannot live immersed in water. If therefore you maintain at one and the same time that the Trumai are men and that they spend some hours every night at the bottom of the water, the logical requirements of your mind differ from those of ours.

But the thought of the Bororo not being conceptual, they escape from this dilemma. Without doubt, they well know that an immersed man drowns and is not long in dying from asphyxia. None of them imagines that he would be able to sleep at the bottom of the river, and would not risk it. But according to them, the case of the Trumai is different. They spend the nights in the water; it is therefore necessary to conclude simply that, on this point at least, they are not men similar to the Bororo and that they enjoy the faculty or privilege of staying underwater without difficulty. Does not one know that fish do and that there are other amphibious beings? The Bororo do not have the least idea about the physiological conditions of life and in particular of the function of respiration. Fish have the ability to live in water, as birds have that of keeping themselves in the air, and one never asks how that is done. Seeing that is it absurd that some men possess these same abilities? Sorcerers can fly through the air; why might not the Trumai be able to sleep in the water? It is enough that they should be endowed with the necessary ability. Now they have it because in fact they do spend the nights in the water. There is in their claim no stretching of logic, no contradiction.

Bagatelle: March 6th, 1938.

Therefore there is no contradiction in the thought of the Bororo to call attention to here. There would be only if they had our concept of man according to which it is understood that he breathes with his lungs and as a result is asphyxiated in water. If the Trumai were men so defined, and if nevertheless it were asserted at the same time that they pass the nights in the water, it would be unacceptable from a logical point of view. But the Bororo do not do this. They do not have the abstract idea of men with properties which necessarily belong to all the beings denoted by this term. For them the Trumai can therefore very well be men from every other point of view and different only in so much as it is possible for them to breathe in water like fish. The Bororo certainly have no idea about the function of lungs, nor, as a result, of the conditions which render it possible or impossible for this function to be exercised.

Therefore we do not say that in this instance their mind makes less logical demands than ours, but only that it does not think through concepts and that it has other mental habits. From the idea of man which we possess we deduce many things, on account of attributes which past experience, crystallized in language, has taught us to subsume under the word 'man', and each new experience confirms this subsumption and thereby makes our deduction legitimate. The Bororo also indeed form concepts, but they remain ill defined, close to concrete images, and consequently they do not serve as tools for deductions. Such a quality or property is in fact very often met with among men—and likewise in all the natural objects with which they have dealings—but all the same it may be that it does not occur in such a person or in a given group of men, for example among the Trumai. If a belief— which for them has the value of an experience and often is not clearly distinguished from one—assures them that while being men they pass their nights at the bottom of the water, they will accept it without difficuly.

These same mental habits, which stop them deducing from concepts what is necessarily included in them, also prevent them from induction in our fashion. We think that the same causes always produce the same effects, and the effects being given that it is always possible to go back to their causes: it does not seem admissable to us that the laws of nature should contradict themselves (the case of miracles excepted). The primitive mentality also bases its techniques on this regular order which controls the phenomena of nature, and in this sense it is the whole time making inductions which experience in point of fact confirms. But at the same time it allows exceptions to occur and it would never have the idea of denying reality in the name of an inviolable determinism. It knows that animals reproduce themselves by means of impregnation; but if it has some reason for imagining that a woman has conceived while still remaining a virgin, it will not dream of rejecting the idea as false and inadmissible.

Briefly, the attitude of primitive mentality as far as it concerns induction is the same as that which concerns deduction. It does not apprehend laws any more than it does concepts. It conforms to the order of nature in its activities: indeed it has to, on pain of disappearing, as animals must also in the more restricted nature they inhabit. But from this practical knowledge of animals (finding food and shelter, fleeing from their enemies, etc.) we do not conclude that they may have the least idea of nature, nor that their thought is governed by logical principles. The case of man is different. He deduces and he induces. The primitive mentality does it differently from ours; it has different mental habits: it is these habits which it is necessary to penetrate.

Parc de Saint-Cloud: March 8th, 1938.

[The whole of this discussion (pp. 125–7 is to be found revived and developed in *Notebook VII*, and is better located under the examination of the formula 'the primitive mentality is not conceptual like ours'—that is to say of the idea that it is formed from the nature of its laws and exceptions to these laws, from its constancy and its fluidity, in brief from the intertwining of positive experience and mythic experience.

October 30th, 1938.]

MYSTICAL EXPERIENCE AND LOGICAL REQUIREMENTS

There cannot be insupportable incompatibilities in experience for minds which are always ready to accept as possible exceptions to and departures from the laws. Evident logical incompatibility —contradiction—is naturally rejected by their mind as it is by ours. But if an exception occurs, if an expected phenomenon does not appear after its normal antecedents, primitive minds will not be shocked because nature for them is not independent of the supernatural.

In brief, if there is for them as for us a logical impossibility, there is no longer *a priori* a physical one. In other words, they bring into contact with the reality of the given world a mind full of mythical thoughts. What would be important and truly original would be to determine what the principles of this mystical thought are, whence they come and how they function; how they acquiesce in the fluidity of things, and whence comes the feeling of participation which they constantly use, without of course formulating it, and might one say, without knowing it. Perhaps from the solidarity of individuals with their group and of appurtenances with the individuals (possessive pronouns).

Bagatelle: March 13th, 1938.

Thus it seems as if in order to explain the mystical character of the primitive mentality I have had to show how their experience is wider than ours, how the experience that I have called mystical is constantly intertwined with that which we have in common with them, yet it is the same mystical experience that allows an explanation of the 'prelogical' character, or of what I have called in too imprecise a way, the lesser logical requirements. This becomes clear if one considers myths. So extraordinary as they often appear to us, so irreconcilable with coherent thought— it is no less true, according to the remark of von den Steinen, that the elements of these myths originate in experience—what other origin could they have?—and that the form and the base are only separable through abstraction. What von den Steinen has not seen, or at least not said, is that this experience differs from ours in this respect, that it also comprises mystical experience and as a result provides facts and connections between these facts which we consider as absurd, unacceptable and incompatible, that is to say impossible in the physical if not the logical sense of the word.

Thus the circle closes again. To say that for them mystical experience is a real experience comes down to saying that their mind has not the same exigencies as ours, or in yet other words that myths are true histories. The reasons which make such facts or such connections unacceptable in our eyes have not the same force for the primitive mentality because of different habits; but, in referring to these habits of thought, we can understand the primitive mentality's position and way of taking things, of not doubting their possibility.

Two elements arise directly, of which I have often indicated the role and the importance: first, the affective category of the supernatural of which the function is specified in Volume VI and which manifests itself constantly in the mystical experience; and second, the imperceptible passage from belief to experience. So imperviousness to experience is only another aspect of the 'prelogical' character of the primitive mentality in so far as, having no need to submit traditional beliefs to criticism nor question whether they are acceptable, it maintains the same attitude with respect to experiences which are not distinguished from beliefs.

Bois de Boulogne: March 21st, 1938.

PARTICIPATION, APPURTENANCES (PRONOUNS)

Thus three points seem to take shape which would furnish material for as many articles, of unequal length, and between which I do not seek to establish connection in advance—there will always be time to study the relations among them if interesting reasons to claim as much should appear.

First. To determine the particular characteristics of the various sorts of participation which until now I have not sufficiently differentiated. For example, the participation between an individual and his appurtenances indeed seems to be of a special nature; what is given or thought or felt in the first place is not the individual (without his appurtenances) and the appurtenances in so far as they exist apart from that individual (hair, saliva, sweat, etc.); it is the totality (one cannot say the synthesis or the union because that would clearly imply that they are at first given separately) of the individual and of the appurtenances unseparated in the feeling of them that one has. In other words, when we speak of participation we oppose this mode of action of the primitive mentality to our own, and in so doing and whether we like it or not we change what is participation for the primitive mentality before we compare it with our idea of participation. In order to be more faithful to the primitive mentality, it would be necessary to feel that the appurtenances are integral parts of the individual, and that it is in virtue of subsequent participations or of a beginning of reflection that they become detached from him. Originally what is felt is what I have called a consubstantiality.

How should we represent to ourselves the fact that a consubstantiality is felt? Naturally we do not have evidence on this point, and if we had it would not perhaps be very reliable. But we are able to develop an idea from a fact of language which is almost universal. In the great majority of primitive languages, the parts of the body, the organs are never found without possessive pronouns—which besides are often simply the personal pronouns. There is never found in the Melanesian or American languages, finger, eye, foot, etc.: it is the finger, the foot or the eye of someone; my foot, or yours, or theirs. *Natugu-gu* includes a personal or possessive pronoun: I, me. Finger-me equals mine, never *natu* all alone. The idea of finger, independent of the person or animal whose finger it is, is not given to begin with, it is the product of a generalization, of an abstract idea. The primitive mentality indeed recognizes a finger of an adult, of a child, of a monkey, of a bear, but while giving it a name which certainly proves that it has the idea in recognizing it, it does not think of the finger on its own. It seems likely that this may be the way that we must represent the relationship of the individual and his appurtenances before, as it were, the separate representation of each of them.

As one knows, the same linguistic fact applies to kinship relations.

From this are to be derived important consequences throwing light on the mental habits of primitive men—in particular it appears that originally they do not represent individuals as such: they never represent them other than as concrete parts of a group to which they 'belong', this is the appropriate word, the organ with the body, the son or brother with the family, etc., like the grape with the bunch. The representation of a separate individual, which seems to us so simple and so natural, is nevertheless not a primitive one. It occurs only secondarily and never alone: without doubt there are individuals—people who belong to the group—but as there are fingers or toes which form part of the hand or foot which in turn forms part of the man who himself forms part of the social group while it above all forms part of the totemic essence. To show how much this mental attitude differs from ours (myths).

Bois de Boulogne: March 22nd, 1938.

A hand detached from the wrist, that is to say from the living body, is no longer a hand; it is a piece of solid and liquid matter which no longer deserves that name. (Aristotle.) The hand is only represented and thought of with the body of which it is a part and which without it is still thinkable and representable, although mutilated. Likewise the member of the clan, or of the sib, of the horde, etc., separated from the social body to which he belongs suffers the same depreciation as the severed hand: he is no more than an individual capable still of movement, sensations, etc., but he has lost his essential determining attribute: he is no longer a member of the tribe as the severed hand does not remain an organ.

If we take this consideration entirely seriously, a quantity of details of the life and thought of primitive men reveals itself in a new light. To begin with, the importance, or better put the necessity of initiation, for without it the individual is not integrated into the group, and the group lacking the initiates would be condemned to disappear. Then when death separates from the group of the living one of its members, he must, in all necessity, be joined to the group of the dead; failing which his existence loses all significance, as, again, the hand separated from the arm. From this arises, in so many societies—primitive and others—the absolute obligation of funerary rites. The dead, no more than the living, cannot do without initiation: if they are denied it they are at the depth of misfortune, and they may also be angry with the living, that is to say dangerous.

At the same time, one takes better account of the feelings which death inspires in them. Do they fear it? Yes, and no. They do not have, as in our societies, the fear of ceasing to be, of falling into nothingness, of being purely and simply removed from the number of the existing at the same time as from the number of the living. They do not even seem to imagine anything of this sort: death is a displacement; the person affected crosses the bridge.

Accordingly there is no metaphysical terror. But all the same he
fears this abrupt change of condition. He is going to continue to
exist elsewhere: will he find there the place which he ought to
occupy? Will he be well received? Will someone look after him,
etc.? (Data from New France.) It is necessary that his personal
status among the 'other members of the clan' in any case be
established, so affirming that he was from this side of the bridge.

March 23rd, 1938.

TO BE, TO EXIST, IS TO PARTICIPATE

Thus I find myself led by the facts to an unexpected conclusion
which I believe to be right. Will something come of it? I cannot
foresee that, but, in any case, it is worth the trouble to note what
I establish, and to do so with the greatest possible precision and
exactness.

It seems to me that one is obliged to admit that in the mind
of the primitive man there are two representations of the surrounding reality which do not coincide, which are even distinctly
different although he is not aware of it. The first is closely linked
to action and is imposed, so to speak, by the imperative needs of
life. Just as in order for an animal species to exist, it is necessary
that each creature be capable, to a certain degree below which it
would certainly disappear, of discerning the objects and things
which are necessary for him to feed himself, protect himself, to
avoid his enemies, etc.: all representations which realize themselves and order themselves in the animal without its having any
need to think about them, and without its even knowing that
there is a representation, this mental activity being required like
the physiological activity when it breathes, digests, etc.—likewise,
for primitive man, whose nourishment and need to escape from
wild beasts and enemies are the constant and so to speak vital
preoccupation, it is necessary to admit a mental activity comparable with that of the animal although already more complex
and richer. Like the animal, he needs a fast and exact perception
of the objects and beings which concern his existence, and this
perception also occurs without there being the need to reflect on
it or even being aware of it. If he finds himself in the presence of
a snake, of a deer, of a tiger, of an edible fish, of a cayman, if he

finds in the forest a bees' nest or some berry which he eats, this familiar perception is generally followed by the appropriate reaction. From this point of view, which I would willingly call bio-psychological, has he properly the idea of the order which comprises these things which concern him and immediately trigger off his action? It is difficult to say, precisely because the interest which they awaken in him is mainly, but that is not to say exclusively, practical. What he perceives arouses in him a complex of emotion and representation in which the emotion dominates; and the necessity to act monopolizes the attention; this last, polarized so to speak by the vital necessities, does not in the animal turn at all on the representation itself.

In man, as in the animal, there is no doubt that this complex also occurs. But there exists also in primitive man another representation of the things and objects in the surrounding environment, in complexes which also include some emotional elements but which differ profoundly from the bio-psychological complexes which also occur in the animal. A characteristic trait of the complexes, perhaps their basic trait, is that the individual beings or objects are only represented in a totality of which they are, if not the parts, at least the integral elements, the constituents, or the replicas. For example, the other individuals who form part of the social group of which the primitive man is a member are in the first place only represented in his mind as members of this group on which he feels that their existence depends, their reality results from participation in the invisible and timeless essence of the group, in a large number of societies in the totem of his clan. Likewise an animal or tree is represented only as a participation in a common essence, sometimes realized in the form of a *boss* or *owner* of the species: and this second representation also has a practical importance as is proved by the magical techniques of hunting, fishing, etc.

Bois de Boulogne: March 23rd, 1938.

Here is a remark which may reduce the difficulties which we have with the participations to which the primitive mentality adapts itself very easily. Despite all our efforts, we do not understand how things which are distinct and separate from each other nevertheless participate with one another, sometimes to the point that they form only one (bi-presence, duality-unity, consubstantiation). But these arise from mental habits different among us and them. For the primitive mentality *to be is to participate*. It does not represent to itself things whose existence it conceives without bringing in elements other than the things themselves. They are what they are by virtue of participations: the member of the human group through participation in the group and in the ancestors; the animal or plant through participation with the archetype of the species, etc. . . . If participation were not established, already real, the individuals would not exist. Thus the question is not: here are objects, individuals, how can they participate with each other? (a problem for which we have no satisfactory solution—except metaphysical to avoid saying mythical); but rather how some clearly defined individuals and, in certain cases, some people disengage themselves from these participations? (Leenhardt.) The answer—by the development of a more and more conceptual thought, by the substitution little by little of the affective with logical abstraction.

Bois de Boulogne: March 30th, 1938.

ACTIONS, STATES, CONCEPTS (SOMMERFELT)

Sommerfelt reaches the very interesting conclusion that the Aranta language, more archaic than any other he knows, than the Ur-Indo-European, has as a characteristic to express only actions and states, but not objects (nor qualities objectively represented). In a different way, and with a precision guaranteed by the language, this is what I indicated as early as *How Natives Think* in which I said that the mental activity of primitive men is not conceptual. Sommerfelt renders this idea differently: objects, he says, are what they are, and nothing else; whereas states and actions are not so 'limited' (I would rather say 'defined') and this last term immediately reminds one of the concept to which clearly corresponds a definition—Further, states and actions necessarily involve a subject, who carries out or undergoes the action at a given moment and place; it is a question of a concrete reality. The same remark applies to states. These characteristics are far removed from those of concepts (abstraction, indefinite applicability, extemporality, etc.). Minds which thus lay stress only on the concrete clearly only think by means of complexes in which the particular representation which has arrested them is mixed with affective and motory elements. Study this form of reality.

Bagatelle: April 16th, 1938.

CASES IN FRENCH WEST AFRICA: INDIFFERENCE TO CAUSE

The case of Fatoumata [and] Sokona, so instructive in various ways, is particularly interesting at the point where the administrator tries to understand the apparently inexplicable attitude of the father, and asks him to explain how, having himself buried his daughter, he could come and complain that she had been stolen and eaten. When the white man tries to show him the contradiction, or at very least the physical incompatibility between the ways of presenting his child's death and what followed it, he is able only to maintain his assertions: yes, I saw her dead in my house; yes, I buried her in the ground; yes, this skeleton is indeed hers.— But then she has not been stolen, she has not been eaten!—'But yes', he replies without hesitation, 'yes, she has been stolen, and the witches have eaten her!' Unable to extract anything from him, the Administrator sees that it is useless to insist, and the cause moreover is perfectly clear.

But if the black man cannot explain himself and still less analyse himself, is it impossible for us to see why he cannot?

One of his answers puts us on the right track. When he is asked how the accused can have eaten a child who has never been in their hands, he replies that they have done it 'the way that witches do'. This explanation, which is completely inadequate for white men, on the contrary satisfies him fully. If we understand why it satisfies him, we will be approaching our objective.

The starting point is the sudden death of the child. It is thus not natural—that is to say it is due to the supernatural action of a spirit, for example, or of a dead man, or of a witch. The father does not need anyone to direct his suspicions in this direction, but to whom, among the probable authors of the death, is he right to attribute it? According to custom, he consults someone who has contact with the supernatural beings, and who knows how to disclose the actions originating from the other world. He learns from the diviner that there are two women of his village, two witches who are the cause of his child's death. But he does not think of their action in an abstract way, starting with a concept. On the contrary, he continues to conform, without needing to think about it, to tradition. This teaches that witches, to kill their victims, eat them. Thus F. and S. have eaten his daughter; this is the same thing as saying that they have killed her.

 The white man would accept that they have killed her but he rejects the assertion that they have eaten her,—because her body has been buried intact. The black man does not contest this last point, nevertheless he persists in his statement. It must be then that the word 'eat' has a special sense for him. And, in effect, on the one hand witches eat as we do when they take their usual meals with us. But on the other hand, when they exercise their fatal action on a person they 'eat' him without anyone, not even the victim himself, being aware of it, more especially as the death is neither immediate nor sudden. The individual who is 'eaten' continues to come and go, but he is lost, he weakens, and more or less quickly he succumbs. Here the word 'eat' has a mystical sense. The victim is 'eaten' in the spiritual sense of the word.

It seems that one can go a little further. Why is the black man, cornered by the Administrator's questions, incapable of explaining his thoughts to him as I have just done?—Because the distinction between the two senses of the word 'eat' which appears so evident and so important to us, has no interest for him. He will not deny it perhaps if it is explained to him clearly. But he does not do it for himself. Let us not forget that the complex analysed by us is eminently affective. His child's death caused by the witches is a mystical experience of the first order, by which he is violently disturbed and deeply troubled. What holds all his attention and his feelings is the revelation of the fact that his child has just been eaten. How has she been eaten? The question how is not posed in the primitive mentality when the cause in question belongs to the world of mystical experience. It has the power to generate its effect, it generates it: what more is there to ask? The succession of phenomena which result in death has no importance; they are at the very most occasional means or causes. The effect is related to its 'true' cause, by which the action, in the complex, is suffered as if direct even if the effect appears only at the end of a certain time. Whether the witches are anthropophagous in the sense with

which we are familiar, or in the spiritual sense, makes no difference to the black man.

Bois de Boulogne: May 10th, 1938.

The indifference of the native who is content to say that the
witch has 'eaten' his victim, without needing to specify how, is
a particular instance of his constant attitude when it is a question
of the witch's action. If the latter has *doomed* someone, death
will certainly follow. Be it from the bite of a snake, or from a tree
falling, or from a crocodile or a tiger, or a hunting accident, etc.:
it does not matter. All ways are equivalent, because in all of them
the *terminus a quo* is witchcraft, the *terminus ad quem* the death
of the victim. The connection is not important. Certainly death
by a snake-bite is not the same thing as death by falling from a
tree, and the difference does not escape the black man. But in his
eyes the difference is negligible, and it does not arrest his attention
for both are, by the same right, the realization of witchcraft and
they are identified by their common outcome. In this sense, they
are the same thing.

Thus there is a mental habit which we do not have, and which
shocks our mind, making us think that this mentality takes strange
liberties with logic—for how can it identify two processes of
phenomena which are evidently different?

The answer: the primitive mentality identifies them because the
particular content of the processes does not interest it, and because
it considers only the beginning or the end. These last being the
same, the processes, whatever the content may be, are equivalent
because they are interchangeable. The witch has made his victim
be seized by a crocodile but he could have chosen to have him
drowned in the river, or poisoned. His action, under an apparently
different form, would be exactly the same.

This mental attitude indifferent to 'how' is easily observed in
cases such as that of the shark (court case from Guinea). A man
is dead as a result of wounds made by a shark which attacked him
in a pool of water on the beach. There are many witnesses. Some
say that the shark was in reality four or five witches who had put
on the shark's skin in order to kill their victim; others that the
witches had entered the body of a real shark; others finally that
they had commanded the shark to devour the man. The white

investigator seeks to pin down what the witnesses have in mind.
Have they seen a shark attack the man? Have they seen men and
women concealed under a shark skin strike the man with a knife
and shark's teeth set in a handle (after the fashion of the Leopard-
men)? He does not obtain any answer which satisfies him, and it
follows from what the witnesses say that they have not thought
of this distinction: what, for the white man, constitutes different
cases, for them is similar. It is a matter of witches who, to achieve
their ends, have chosen recourse to the shark. Whether they turned
themselves into sharks, or whether they entered an existing
shark, or whether they made a certain shark act as agent of
execution, is all the same thing. I have noted this mental attitude
with reference to the sorcerers of New Guinea who have chosen
rats as the means to achieve their ends (*Primitives and the
Supernatural*). Do they turn themselves into rats? Do they send
the rats to damage the coconuts? The Papuan has no answer to
this question because he has not asked it of himself, and if he is
asked it he is embarrassed. To say that he represents the cases
to himself as being identical would be inexact; that he does not
distinguish between them is closer to the truth; not that he is
incapable of distinguishing between them; but, in fact, he himself
does not know if he is representing to himself one rather than
the other.

Bois de Boulogne: May 11th, 1938.

Notebook II
May-June 1938

It may be asked whence arises such a general indifference in those minds to the variety of ways by which the act of witchcraft attains its end, and how it is that these minds consider processes to be equivalent which to us appear very different: sickness, drowning, falling, etc. . . . To seek the explanation of the nature of the intellectual operations involved would lead nowhere, firstly because in fact there are few intellectual operations in this complex; but principally schemes and memories.

The starting point from which the series of representations and acts departs is significant and suggests the way which may lead to the desired answer. In general it is because something abnormal, or unusual, hence baleful and of bad augury, has happened, and it is necessary, as far as possible, to prevent other misfortunes occurring (*malum augurium*). Thus, in the affair of the shark-witch of Conakry, the origin of the suspicions, accusations and of what ensued is to be found in the fact that, on this beach, no one remembers having seen sharks. Doubtless there are some, even many, at the mouths of neighbouring rivers. But on this beach, there is none. They live in fresh water, not in the sea. Accordingly the presence of a shark is something extraordinary. Thus it is immediately 'felt' as evidence of the presence of the action of a supernatural force. This shark is a witch transformed, or the representative or instrument of a witch (it comes to the same thing).

At the same moment the affective category of the supernatural comes into action, and what is going to follow is determined in advance; a psychic fact having little in common with a truly intellectual activity.

In the first place, the affective elements predominate in the complex. The misfortune that reveals the action of a supernatural and invisible force causes a violent and deep emotion, impossible to disregard, which itself immediately provokes reactions that are rigorously predetermined in their form by the precedents with which the social tradition is full. How, if there is still time, to protect oneself against the harmful action of this power?—Above all to know what one is dealing with. For example, is it a dead man or one or many witches? Hence, the first reaction, to invoke the help of the only members of the group who have access to the supernatural world (diviner, fetisher, medicine man, doctor, etc.). It is up to him to say, for example, who is or who are the witches responsible for what has happened.

In the second place, if it is not too late, to save the member of the group who has been struck. It is characteristic that the sole means in which there is confidence is also drawn from the supernatural world. It is necessary and sufficient that he who cursed the victim lift off the curse. This is why he is forced 1. to confess; 2. to return close to his victim; 3. to carry out on the victim or on his appurtenances acts which are exactly the opposite of the original ones which caused the hurt. Accordingly there is no other causality conceived or imagined than that of the supernatural force connected directly with its effect: for example, the witch's power is the real and *complete* cause of death. For primitive man, this remains true even if the witch summons the help of an animal, or of a vegetable, of any natural object whatever (river, lake or rock) which is at his disposition. The crocodile in the service of the witch does not kill the victim, it has no responsibility. The sole author of the death is the witch who has given this mission to the crocodile. It is this way of apprehending the fact that finds expression in indeterminacy which astonishes us. Is the murderous crocodile an agent of the witch, or is it the witch himself? The native does not know, and does not seek to know. Why? Because in the latter case as in the former there is only a single author of the death; the connection between his action and the result obtained (the death of the victim) being direct, there is no process of phenomena which actually occurs in what happens, despite appearances. *We* believe that the crocodile has caught and devoured the man (cf. Bentley). We are fooled by appearances. The black men know who wanted and obtained his death.

The analysis of the story of Fatoumata and Sokona provides us with exactly the same ingredients. What has been the *primum movens* of the affair? Maliki's child, sick, is 'suddenly' dead. There is something abnormal here, something unusual; immediately the affective category comes into action: all the more easily as the fact of the sickness alone would already suggest the idea of bewitchment. The death which *happens* unexpectedly makes the suspicion a certainty.

Bagatelle: May 12th, 1938.

THE AFFECTIVE CATEGORY OF THE SUPERNATURAL AND CAUSALITY

It is not in the logical modality of mental activity, therefore, that it is necessary to seek the explanation of this indifference to the diversity of processes through which a single result—the death of the bewitched victim—is obtained. To say that these processes are equivalent, interchangeable, for the primitive mentality does not mean that it represents them as identical from the logical point of view, or as similar from the physical point of view (points of view which moreover it is very far from distinguishing). It is to say simply that the primitive mentality does not see any interest in considering the processes: it is indifferent to what characterizes each of them separately because they are indifferent to it; not that it is unaware of the characteristics peculiar to the snake, crocodile, shark, etc., or that it neglects to take account of them when there is occasion to do so, but in the present case the things in question interest primitive man only because of what they have in common and not because of the characteristics peculiar to each—that is to say they interest him only in so far as they are instrumental in the realization of a certain goal. By each of these different ways the goal is attained, and that alone matters to him. What entirely occupies him at the moment is the emotion provoked by the event experienced, by the coming into action of the affective category of the supernatural through the perspective of other misfortunes.

And yet, on the other hand, this is not a matter of a uniquely affective complex. The idea that there is a cause for what has happened, that one knows what species of cause has acted, and the need to try to discover what particular representative of this species of cause is present in this circumstance, are, as much as emotion and fear, in the foreground of consciousness. There is an activity of the mind in so far as there is thinking. The difficulty is to find terms adequate for an exact description. Those which are at our disposal are provided for us by a tradition, the secular work of psychologists and philosophers who have before their eyes a society other than that of black men, and above all are accustomed to study reality by speculating on concepts.

But whatever may be the drawbacks to these terms for what we have to study, it is better to be resigned to them—knowing these drawbacks—than to risk neologisms which would certainly give rise to confusion, to mistakes, and to interminable misunderstandings. It is still the lesser evil. Thus we will say that those black men of French West Africa and primitive men in general submit these cases of witchcraft to a need for causality at the same time as to the emotions which accompany the setting in action of the affective category of the supernatural. This is why the question posed concerns, not exclusively but none the less essentially, the logical aspect of the primitive mentality. It tries to account for what has happened. It needs an explanation, and as long as one is not given it will never be satisfied. Our problem is hence posed in slightly more precise terms, which is an advance, and a necessary though not sufficient condition for an approach to a solution. How is the affective category of the supernatural involved in the elementary demands of the mind in its cognitive capacity, in so far as it feels the need to find the reason for events, to explain things? What are the relations between this affective category and the category of causality?

Two points to consider:

1. The affective category only comes into action when primitive man feels himself in the presence and under the influence of an invisible or supernatural power (even if this reveals itself in a visible form and under a natural guise—(animals which are not really animals)). The category of causality functions—without emotion, and certainly without reflection and awareness just as the digestive, or respiratory systems, etc., function at every moment in the whole course of ordinary experience. But we are also saying that the primitive mentality, indifferent to secondary causes, seeks the true cause elsewhere—thus it is still the category of causality at work.

Bois de Boulogne: May 13th, 1938.

The affective category of the supernatural, in so far as it is not simply affective, i.e. when it comes into action, does not provide knowledge but the feeling (if we distinguish it from emotion properly so called, from which it is inseparable in the complex which occupies the consciousness of the individual) of an active and present being, although this is most often invisible and imperceptible to the sense. It is an ultimate, or, if you like, immediate, datum of the experience that is called mystical, and beyond which I do not see how it would be possible to go.

The question I ask myself is: How is this category which 'gives' an existence involved with the category of causality? What are the relations between them in the primitive mentality as it acts after the observation of the events?

I do not find a satisfying answer, doubtless because the question is badly put and because the terms on the one side and the other do not belong to the same order. The affective category of the supernatural expresses the fundamental character of a certain experience, and it is this character, which is always present when an experience of this type occurs, which justifies the use of the word 'category' (uniformity of emotion and of the datum of existence which invariably accompanies it in the complex, even when the emotion is most acute, this emotion being revealed in itself).

There is nothing epistemological here. On the contrary, as soon as we speak of causality, of the category of causality, we imply the attitude common to the theoreticians of knowledge, whoever they may be: it is impossible to be entirely outside what has been described and analysed from Plato and Aristotle down to Hume and Kant. To obtain, if not an answer, at least a partial solution to the question posed above, it is necessary to start by improving the terms which are brought together.

Now, clearly, there is nothing to change in the terms which designate the affective category of the supernatural since these are they which have appeared to answer best to what has been observed and analysed in the very complex of which it is a question. But for the category of causality we ought to find terms other than those normally used in the theory of knowledge. Is this possible? There are no other means of making sure than by attempting a description and an analysis of the facts which is concerned with them *exclusively* and which is entirely free from all contact with psychological and philosophical speculation on the question and from what is implied by its terminology.

Nevertheless it is indeed necessary to use the word 'cause'. But let us avoid assuming that the primitive mentality uses it with the sense which it has for us, and let us try to define what it means to them (primitive men) when they make use of their corresponding word. From the first one sees: 1. that it does not express the idea of something which, in the mind, may be separated from the complex in which it was included. It is in no way detached from the effect produced by the cause in question, not even from the affective elements which accompany the action of the cause, the outcome of the effect with its consequences for the individual and for the group, etc. Thus, from this point of view, one can speak of the relations of cause to felt effects, and even up to a certain point thought, 'realized' as such, but not of a general representation, even though fairly concrete, of causality as the connecting principle of phenomena.—and 2. it is not at all certain that the relation of cause and effect is felt and thought in the same way when it is a matter of facts *intra naturam*, and when the category of the supernatural is involved.

Brussels: May 17th, 1938.

CAUSALITY IN NATURE ACCORDING TO THE PRIMITIVE
MENTALITY

Let us therefore dismiss, at least provisionally, the representation which is always present in our mind, even if we do not think about it, of the connection of phenomena which are produced by a causal nexus which ensures order; or, in other words, our attitude, so habitual that it is almost instinctive, in the presence of that which experience brings us daily, in the course of the day. In order to realize, as far as possible, the mentality of primitive men, in so far as it differs from ours, let us recall the peculiar characteristics of their experience. It appears to us to be double, though for them it constitutes only a single experience; we see mixed together there an experience similar to ours (same sense data, same perceptions, apprehension of the same sequences of phenomena in the surrounding world), and a mystical experience, an intermittent revelation of an invisible and unknowable reality, of the presence and action of forces and powers from the next world, the spirits, for example, and the dead. The question which then presents itself to us is formulated thus: how does the primitive mentality feel and, at least in certain cases, think of the connection in each of these experiences considered singly and together?

Brussels: May 18th, 1938.

If we consider first the ordinary experience such as that which happens to each of these individuals when nothing disturbs it, or in phenomena the regularity of which never or rarely fails— the succession of nights and days, the course of the sun and the moon, the familiar behaviour of animals which one has observed at all times, the growth of plants, seasonal events, etc.—it seems clear that the primitive mentality immersed in this environment adapts itself to the best of its ability according to the traditional system and thinks no more about it, no longer asks how the regular relationship of phenomena is formed, that it does not perceive atmospheric pressure, nor how it breathes and digests, as long as the functions do not suffer from any trouble. Is this to say that there is nothing in it which corresponds to the unreflecting confidence of our minds (leaving aside any reflection or philosophical speculation) in the certain constancy of the laws of nature?—Like us, when they place a pot full of water on the fire, they expect it to get hot and to end by boiling. For them, as for us, there is a great number of sequences of regular phenomena, and they, like us, count on this regularity. Their practices and techniques are the proof. If, nevertheless, there is a difference between their mental attitude and ours, of what does it consist? This is the real question which is posed for us.

The difference does not appear at once. The Indian or the Papuan takes the regularity of the sequences of phenomena for granted, it seems, as do uneducated minds in all other civilizations. But look at them more closely, and as soon as a departure from the regularity occurs, a difference appears. In our civilizations, save in the very rare case of the miracle, no one thinks that the regularity has ceased to exist, but simply that the phenomenon which occurs is more complicated than one expected, and that one can find the explanation of this unexpected complexity if one tries. The underlying conviction, although unconscious, is that the regularity is belied only in appearance, whereas for primitive man the interruption in the regularity is accepted as real, as is the regularity itself.

Brussels: May 18th, 1938.

MEANING OF 'TRANSFORMATION' FOR THE PRIMITIVE MENTALITY

When I speak, without preliminary criticism, of mental habits among primitive men, which are different from ours, this way of talking involves a parallelism which I have not expressly established and which, thus accepted so to speak *a priori*, risks becoming embarrassing; for it will be asked how the mental habits of 'primitive men' are erased in order to make way for others. A gratuitous difficulty, as is the hypothesis involved in this expression.

It would in fact be an advance if, instead of presupposing these 'mental habits' in primitive men, we abandon the idea, at least provisionally, in order to examine the facts, as much as possible without any preconceived notion. Such, for example, as those which the notes of Mrs. Dugast supply on the subject of leopard-men. At first they give the impression that the ideas of the natives are irremediably confused. The leopard-man at certain times is transformed into a leopard, but he himself is also a leopard, or he has *his* leopard which is at his service, and he dies when it dies, etc. . . . These facts are not new: they repeat those which I have noted among the Naga, among the Papuans of New Guinea, etc., and this concordance (it would be easy to lengthen the list) is already in itself significant.

Either the Papuan witches transform themselves into rats which damage the coconuts, or they send rats to do the damage. Either the African witch causes his victim to be seized by a real crocodile on his orders, or he is himself that crocodile. Even if he has the choice between two ways of achieving his aim, he still must decide between them. When he has chosen one, the other, clearly (for us), is excluded. Now it is remarkable that for the primitive man it is not a case of *entweder* [either] . . . *oder* [or]. If the question is put to him, often he cannot say which of the ways of acting has been chosen. The question does not interest

him. He knows that the witch, at his will, can as well choose
one as the other. The power and the action of the witch are
alone important to him. What holds our attention is unimportant
to him.

In order to understand this indifference, which surprises us,
it is necessary to give up the representation that we have of men
and animals and to renounce affectively the concepts which we
have formed of them—or at least to approach as near as possible
a representation without concept. Perhaps the following way
might allow it. In the eyes of primitive man the witch has the
power to turn himself into a leopard, that is to say one now sees
him in human form; a few minutes ago one saw him in the form
of the leopard, and perhaps he is going to resume that form in a
moment. This transformation takes place as soon as he enters
the skin of the leopard, and ceases as soon as he leaves it (for
primitive men a change of skin is equivalent to a change of body).
In short, in successive moments, the witch is either man or else
leopard. It is probable that, if he wished, he might be another
animal or a plant or some other thing. Primitive man does not
see any difficulty here: the myths have taught him, and he is
[accordingly] convinced, that the form of individuals is only
an accident. What matters is the *power to take* this or that
form.

Consequently, between these two assertions: 'Such a man is at
will a man or a leopard' and 'Such a man is a leopard, or a
leopard-man', the real difference, which is considerable for us, is
not so for the primitive mentality. It is so small a matter that for
him (primitive man) it barely exists. The man who in a minute
will be a leopard and some moments afterwards will become a
human again undergoes, according to us, transformations so
profound that they are simply unbelievable. For the primitive
mentality (the form being only an accident) the transformation
is only an apparent, superficial change, a change of skin (let us
recall the eagles, the king vultures which put on and take off
their bird costumes). As much as to say that it is not a matter of
transformation, in the sense which we use, in which we cannot
but use the word.

Accordingly, it makes no difference to say that the man
becomes a leopard or that he is a leopard. He, who in the twink-
ling of an eye becomes a leopard, is already a leopard. To be the

two successively is no different from being the two simultaneously. Hence the constant mental attitude of primitive men on this point which is so difficult for us to grasp and moreover to hold onto for a time (application in the case of the shark-witch from the neighbourhood of Conakry).

One sees immediately that this attitude would not be possible if those minds had the *intellectual* usage of the concept of man, of the concept of animal, of leopard, crocodile, rat, etc. . . . In fact, in their *behaviour* everything happens as if they had this concept. There is no reason to deny that they possess it at all. They make practical use of it (animals also have something which approaches it although distantly). Since man has language he expresses these concepts, like us, and we are led to think that they possess them as we do and use them as we do. Here is the mistake which the above facts reveal.

Bois de Boulogne: June 3rd, 1938.

CONCEPTS WITH AND WITHOUT PERSPECTIVE

Let us try to define a little better what these general ideas or representations of things (animals, plants, stones, objects) are in the mentality of primitive men, and free ourselves as far as possible from the framework of traditional psychology, and at the same time from the inevitable implications which result from its terminology: for example, if we use the word 'concept' when it is a matter of those general ideas in primitive men, let us not claim *ipso facto* for their minds what concepts imply in ours.

When they perceive a tree, a bird, a fish, etc., there are clearly some common elements between their representation and ours, and one can try to separate them in order to disengage those elements which are taken to be proper to them and those on the other hand to us. The essential common element is the recognition of an individual or object of which the experience is familiar to the subject (an element present even if the individual or object is unusual, for without it the experience of the unusual would perhaps be impossible). The subject perceives at the same time the individual or object, having often seen others like it, and the name of the individual or object immediately leaps to mind. Does this name express a concept, and if so, is the concept in every way similar to those that we employ the whole time? If not, what is the difference, and how great is it?

Let us start by considering the corresponding phenomenon among animals which do not have speech. They also 'recognize' certain things and objects in their surroundings, and often with great shrewdness and exactness. It is indeed necessary for them to distinguish those which they use for food, their prey, their enemies, for failing this they would quickly succumb and the species would disappear. But to what extent is it a question here of a psychic phenomenon properly so called, of a 'recognition' of a fact of memory, implying the presence if not of a general idea at least of a generic image, it is difficult to say, and it would need an especially detailed study, in particular of the species which have the most developed mental life. For others, the sensible impression produced by such or such a thing determines above all a reflex of flight, of attack, or of movement, tending to assure the safety or well-being of the animal. When the warning sense is the sight, we have a tendency to accept in the animal a visual perception which consists of an image and that this image immediately recalls similar images from its earlier experience—consequently the presence in it of a sort of generic idea which makes this comparison possible.

But perhaps this is an unwarranted hypothesis, into which we are led by the analogy between what happens in such cases in the animal and what happens in man. If the presumed 'recognition' is made, not by a visual or auditory perception, but by an impression due to another sense, by smell for example, we do not think so naturally and immediately of a generic 'image', nor even of an image properly so called, and the question arises of knowing if one ought to speak of 'recognition' or simply of a reflex which is set in motion, without doubt a reflex more complex than those of higher animals, and implying some psychic elements which in these last do not seem to come into play—but all the same fitting into the class of phenomena designated by the term 'reflex'.

A remark supporting the above statement: the reflex is set in motion only on well defined occasions. The surrounding environment gives rise, for the animal, to a multitude of sensible impressions and perceptions at least in the nascent state. The animal seems interested in only a small number from among these, in general those which provide something favourable or

unfavourable in the normal action of its functions or which strike
it by their unusual character. As for the rest, it shows itself particularly indifferent: things and objects are for it as if they did not
exist. Impressions are formed on its sense, and are certainly transmitted. Whether there is perception, and to what extent it is
subconscious or conscious, we do not know; but what we see is
that the animal does not appear to pay the slightest attention.
Thus there is no ground for supposing that there is formed in it
a generic image of these things and objects in the sensed presence
of which (if it is truly sensed) it does not react in any way
(curiosity in some species).

Even in the most 'primitive' man whom we may be able to
observe, things happen in a very different way. As in animals,
particularly the higher animals, certain impressions and perceptions determine immediately the 'recognition' of things and
objects; the reaction which follows more or less quickly is accompanied, even if it is very quick and as if instantaneous, by a
psychic complex in which the image of the object with the
affective phenomena which it ordinarily creates has a central
place, and most often we would be hard put to it to trace a line
of demarcation between what it is right to call a generic image
and a general idea. In fact there is an infinity of degrees and
insensible transitions. According to the necessities of the fight for
life, the images can vary greatly in the exactness and precision of
detail. For example, one knows that many 'primitive men' are
capable of distinguishing among the fruits and tubers on which
they live a considerable number of species, sub-species and
varieties: this supposes the minute comparison of images which
are often fairly close to one another, and decisions resulting from
this comparison. Of course, nothing authorizes us to suppose that
there exists in each 'primitive man' who can distinguish these
varieties the operations of comparison and judgement, nor that
he is aware of them; he has learned from his seniors to perceive
these distinctions, and he is simply using the store of traditional
knowledge. But it is indeed necessary to admit: 1. that the
establishment of these traditions of subtle distinctions is a specifically human phenomenon, which supposes something more than
the generic images of animals or their 'general ideas', if it is
accepted that they have them, and 2. that one does not see how
the generic images or the general ideas might be formed, pre-

served, and transmitted in even the most rudimentary human societies if they did not possess language.

From the sole fact that these varieties, for example, have each received a name, what they have in common and what each has which is its own is fixed: when a variety of such a plant is perceived, *ipso facto* its name arising in the mind of the men who perceives it releases the characteristic generic image which the variety traditionally designates, and the image thus finds itself placed in the full light of awareness, which at the same moment makes possible the customary reaction in similar cases. It seems difficult not to recognize in this an idea, and even, however weak may be the difference between the varieties, a general idea since it is a *pattern* which fits all the individuals of this variety which are of an indefinite number and of which new examples can always appear, to which the native will immediately apply their name.

This process in 'primitive man' therefore differs essentially from that which, as a result of the same sensible impression, is produced in the animal. But is it in primitive man exactly similar to that which is produced in our societies? Let us not be too hasty in claiming as much, as we are tempted to do, because we admire the acuteness of the differentiation made between perceived things and objects, in certain cases, by 'primitive men' and the exuberant richness of their vocabulary on these occasions. It is possible that the results which they obtain in such cases (may be) as detailed and exact as ours, (but that) they may be reached by other routes. In any case it is worth the effort to examine the question. We can draw some undue conclusions from the fact that they seem to use as we do the resources which language provides. Are we right in asserting that their general ideas may be similar to ours, and interact together as they do in us? Do they imply, in the way that we are used to, that their extension and inclusion are taken into account, and that their relations suppose a more or less rudimentary classification which is founded on an observable and observed order?

As usual, we will not seek the answer to the question by the dialectical method; we will try to find it in the observation and analysis of the facts. In the first place, one observation has often been made. These same natives who have some forty or sixty names to designate varieties of fruits or plants (of palms, for

example, or yams), often do not have words to designate the
family or species to which the varieties belong. They have a word
for all the varieties of a certain palm but none to designate the
palm in general as they have names for such and such part of the
course of a river but none for the river itself. But one must not
be fooled by appearances. They do not differentiate species by
reference to the genus in which they include them while at the
same time distinguishing them, nor the subspecies in the species,
nor the varieties in the subspecies, etc. . . . What interests them,
what matters to them, is to know how to recognize the objects
without confusing them with each other, the distinction being of
great advantage for them in action, and for this recognition it is
enough for them to have a precise image of all the characteristics
proper to the species or variety concerned without being concerned with the degree of generality of the characteristics, which
for us (even for people without scientific knowledge) subordinates
them to each other. They do not pay attention to their respective
importance, any more than, when they describe a state or action,
they neglect details which our languages no longer contain
(examples of American languages in *How Natives Think*). In
other words their generic images are without perspective. From
this we can infer that, even if their general ideas are expressed by
the same words as ours—they say as we do an elephant, a crocodile, a yam, a taro, etc.—this identity of vocabulary does not prove
that their general ideas are concepts like ours.

But, it might be said, they also have their classifications, which
introduce order while differing from ours: for example, the
Indians of North America who distinguish plants which grow at
the water's edge, or the Australians who have at least the rudi-
ments of a system like the classes of the Bantu languages: round
things, long things, angular things, etc. . .—This sort of classification applies exclusively to the memory, and is born of an
activity of the mind similar to that from which arises the extreme
complication of detail of the verbs mentioned above. It is a matter
of something pictorial: the expression disregards nothing that
serves to characterize the generic image of individuals and objects
—but this generic image is little suited to a logical usage which
would permit the subordination of one to another in such a way
as to make it unnecessary actually to evoke them in order to recall
them: if this subordination existed, the name alone would be

enough for this evocation and the logical operation would become possible. In brief, the general ideas of these minds *partake more of the generic image than of the concept.*

   Varengeville: June 6–8th, 1938.

MODIFIED POSITIONS AND EXPRESSIONS

Before starting on the analysis of some African materials it will not be unprofitable to note where I stand since I began to try and refine what I called in *How Natives Think* and afterwards the prelogical character of the primitive mentality when I saw the misunderstandings which this expression caused, which signifies the fact that this mentality has not 'the same exigencies as ours', or that it is not as sensitive as ours to contradiction, and that in certain circumstances at least it accommodates itself to contradictions which we do not tolerate.

After what has been revealed and analysed in *La Mythologie Primitive*, and in *L'Expérience Mystique et les Symboles chez les Primitifs* I will no longer express myself in that manner. Above all I will no longer place, so to speak, on an equal level the two fundamental characteristics of the primitive mentality, prelogical and mystical, as I did in *How Natives Think*. It now appears that there is a single fundamental characteristic, namely the mystical; the other which I had believed ought to be associated with it, as no less essential, the prelogical, appears henceforth as another aspect or rather as a natural consequence of the first.

If this is the case, first of all it is necessary to say it expressly, if only to show where a less incomplete knowledge of the facts and a more mature and deeper reflection on them have led me, and then to justify this change in position, or at very least of language, it is necessary to recapitulate successively the reasons (that is to say the facts) which were my grounds for asserting the 'prelogical' character of the primitive mentality, and to show how it is explained by the mystical character of that mentality: for example, how it tolerates contradictions that our mind immediately rejects; —how it appears under certain circumstances to lack the sense of the impossible (mythical transformations taken for events which have happened, which still actually happen—the Trumai who sleep at the bottom of the river—indifference to the chain of

secondary causes as soon as it is a matter of a mystical experience);—how it admits without difficulty the facts of bi- or
multipresence, of duality-unity;—how it is satisfied with participations which it often feels as real without caring to know whether
they are intelligible, possible. In Volumes I–VI these questions
have been touched upon very often, but I related them to a
particular character of the primitive mentality. Now it is a matter
of putting these questions properly and discussing them.

Évian: June 15th, 1938.

A change of expression, corresponding to a greater precision
and to a better interpretation of better known facts, would have
at least two great advantages:

1. It would put an end to serious misunderstandings which I
have never been able to dispel entirely and for which the 'prelogical' character of primitive mentality in *How Natives Think*
had furnished a plausible pretext. I have had the approbation of
many colonials,—but many have refused to follow me, many of
them English, and they have not changed their attitude despite
my explanations. This is because it is clear to them that the
human mind is everywhere the same and they find that it is not
necessary to waste their time discussing the contrary thesis, which
they attribute to me. I still recall Colonel Bertrand (brother-in-law
of Hostelet) who had spent many years in the Belgian Congo, and
who protested to me simply: 'But no, you are wrong, those people
think like us.' In renouncing the characterization of the primitive
mentality as prelogical I pacify these contradictors and moreover
I have some chance of inducing them to pay attention to the rest
of what I have said; in general, they are not enchanted with the
'mystical' character, but they have not rejected it outright like
'prelogical'.

2. I have always conceded to Colonel Bertrand and those who
think like him that in a host of circumstances, in daily life, in a
large number of political, economic relations, etc., the primitive
mentality displays no prelogicality; they proceed as we do, and
one can foresee the processes which take place in their minds.
But in other circumstances (for example, when they are in the
presence of a mystical experience, accident, sickness, suspicion of
witchcraft, bi-presence, etc.) I have insisted on the 'prelogical'

nature of these processes. And then it may be asked of me: Where is the boundary between these two aspects of the same mentality, sometimes logical like ours, sometimes prelogical? How does it cease to be logical or prelogical? It is impossible to claim a mentality that is peculiar to primitive men and to them alone, and still more to distinguish between societies in which the primitive mentality dominates and others; the list to be drawn up would be discouraging. It is no less difficult to separate the logical from the prelogical in a human head. In brief, it is time to draw for myself the conclusions which follow from *La Mythologie Primitive* and above all from *L'Expérience Mystique et les Symboles chez les Primitifs*, and which call for a rectification in the way of presenting what I had to say.

Évian: June 17th, 1938.

In fact, for at least twenty years, I have made no further use of 'prelogical', which has caused me so much bother. I have replaced it by some less compromising expressions: 'These minds do not have, in some given circumstances, the same logical requirements as ours'—'they are differently oriented'—'they have different mental habits'.

It seems that as I have employed other expressions I have little by little tempered, attenuated, the difference which I thought I had established between the primitive mentality and ours, from the logical point of view. In *How Natives Think* this difference is outstanding, clearly self-evident, and I assert it with force; the primitive mentality is opposed to the other as essentially different, and even though I recognized at the same time the fundamental identity of the structure of all human minds—all capable of reasoning, of speaking, of counting, etc.—I am reproached endlessly for the contrast which I sought to establish between the mental functions of primitive men and ours. The attenuations which I have made little by little to the thesis of *How Natives Think* have not been of much service. And in effect I have not retracted it though renouncing it. The question thus remains. How do I now characterize the primitive mentality from the logical point of view?

Évian: June 19th, 1938.

E

FACTS FROM FRENCH WEST AFRICA: MINDS OTHERWISE
ORIENTED

Characteristic facts which allow the understanding of the precise
difference between the mental activity of primitive man and of us
on a given point. They are set out, without any attempt at
interpretation, in documents relating to French West Africa: they
form part of legal depositions and interrogations.

1. The case of Damayé Samara, 1927–8, on the outskirts of
Conakry. H. is attacked and wounded by a crocodile; very
unusual occurrence. The village chief calls a witch-doctor who
discovers the culprits. Confessions. Condemnation not officially
confirmed: additional information, decisive report from the doctor
at Conakry hospital. New discussions. Impossible to make the
accused understand that certain hypotheses are mutually exclusive, and that it is necessary to choose. Either it was a real
crocodile, or the culprit had transformed himself into a crocodile
in order to attack the man—or the culprits, hidden under a
crocodile's skin and crawling in the mud, have attacked the man
with crocodile's teeth embedded in a piece of wood and with a
knife. No means of making them understand the incompatibility.
They have acted 'in the way witches do'. There is no need to
know more: the 'how' of this occurrence is of no concern to them
(90–8).

2. The case of Fatoumata Mandi and Sokona Sampon. French
Guinea, region of Boké (1929). Impossible to make the victim's
father, who has seen his daughter dead in her hut, who has even
buried her himself, who has directed the exhumation, to understand that she was not kidnapped and eaten by the two witches
whom the witch-doctor has detected; he holds to his opinion like
Grubb's Indian. Insensible to the *entweder-oder* (46–66).

3. An entirely analogous case from the same region of Boké:
the kidnapping of a child in order to eat him. The mother, an
accomplice, took part in the meal. Improbable confessions.
Stubborness of the father who claims at one and the same time
that he saw and that he did not see. Condemnation. Judgement
not officially confirmed. Additional information. The confessions
were false. The remains are found (66–71).

4. Again from the same region of Boké (1935). A man leaving

the paddy field is bitten on the leg by a snake and dies almost immediately. It does not seem natural. Accordingly it is necessary to discover the witch. The witch-doctor is called in. Denunciation by the piece of cotton-flannel which is never wrong. It indicates the culprits who have wanted Issifou's death. Five accused are brought to justice. Statements and interrogations entirely characteristic. The accused Koufory has killed Issifou by means of the *bingo* (magical little gun as large as the hand which throws wooden needles); he turned himself into a snake in order to bite Issifou; he caused him to be bitten by a snake under his orders. Impossible to get the witnesses who have given successively these different versions, to say which is the truth; furthermore these witnesses incidentally avow that they did not *see*. But they are no less sure of what they claim; and are insensible to the incompatibility of their claims (38–45).

These three incidents, so clear, occuring in less than sixteen years in a single region of French Guinea, allow one to think that a number of other very similar cases must have happened in the area which have not been known about or of which the singularities and impossibilities have passed unnoticed. Fantastic confessions, through fear or even out of good faith; lack of concern about the methods of the bewitching (cf. the rats of Landtman).

Évian: June 20th, 1938.

From cases of this sort, which are numerous, where primitive men show themselves indifferent to incompatibilities which are evident in our eyes, must it be inferred that, in these circumstances, the logical requirements of their mind are less than that of ours, as I have asserted, and what must be understood exactly by that?

In the first place, it is not correct that, left to themselves, they show themselves indifferent to the incompatibility of two facts of which they affirm simultaneously the reality. They are neither indifferent nor the opposite: they do not perceive it. Why?—not through logical weakness, but because, at such moments, they are oriented otherwise. As soon as the suspicion of witchcraft has taken hold of them, the affective category of the supernatural comes into action, and they find themselves transported on to the

level of mystical experience. Whether it is a real crocodile under
the orders of the witch, or the witch himself disguised as a
crocodile, it is the same thing. One has left the domain of ordinary
experience, one is in the presence of a mystical experience in the
domain of supernatural forces. The attention is focused on the
supernatural force, and has no cause to look for the means which
the supernatural force employs, since it has everything which it
wants at its disposal. Complex above all affective.

Évian: June 20th, 1938.

EXPERIENCE OF PRIMITIVE MEN LESS HOMOGENEOUS THAN
OURS

2. What raises some more important and more difficult questions
is how is it, when a flagrant incompatibility in their assertions has
been pointed out to them, that they seem not to perceive it better,
and are incapable of deciding between the claims that cannot be
maintained together? Maliki himself buried his daughter, and
recognizes her when she is exhumed. He continues none-the-less
to maintain that she had been stolen and eaten. In despair of
reason the president of the tribunal abandons the case. How to
explain Maliki's state of mind?

If it seems to us more than strange and incomprehensible, it is
not that their logical requirements are less exacting than ours
and that they are less sensitive to contradiction: an explanation
which I have given, but which I now judge inadequate. It is
because, inadvertently, I assume implicitly that these minds are
oriented like mine, and that their experience is essentially of the
same type as ours. Now it is otherwise in this circumstance. Their
mind is oriented mystically and where for us it is a matter of a
homogeneous and ordinary experience only, it is for them a
matter of an experience, at one and the same time, ordinary and
mystical, in which they do not think to separate what conforms to
the natural order from what depends on supernatural forces.

For us, the necessity to choose between the two incompatible
assertions flows from the fact that both relate to the naturally
perceived reality. The child has been stolen and eaten: this is an
event which can be seen by witnesses, which leaves some traces,
which can be verified. The child is dead in her hut, the father

has buried her. This is a fact which also had witnesses and which is verified by exhumation. While it is a matter of the same child, the facts cannot be right in both cases. Thus we would like the father (and the other natives) to admit that the first is false, that the witnesses who affirmed it have lied, or have been fooled by an illusion. We do not understand their reluctance. Now, not only do they hesitate, but they refuse to heed us, and however well established may be the second case they do not abandon the first.

Thus it is necessary to try to adopt their mental attitude, instead of attributing ours to them. Their experience in this case is not homogeneous and on a single plane, as we imagine it. Death of the child, burial of the corpse, exhumation: all this is indeed an object of actual or possible perception for them as for us. But the disappearance of the child, from the act of witches who kidnapped her in order to eat her soul, takes place on the level of the supernatural, and can be perfectly real without being in the least degree perceived. The incompatibility, therefore, is not flagrant for them as it is for us; the facts do not exclude each other, because they are not on the same level of homogeneous experience perceptible to the senses.

Given that, it matters little that in their evidence the self-styled witches recount how they have carried off and killed the child, cooked and ate her, speak of the cooking-pot, and meat put on one side, etc. . . . All this, which our positive mind takes literally, has only a figurative sense for the mind of primitive men. We give to the words kidnap, kill, eat only a single, univocal sense. For primitive men the sense is double: that which indicates a well known action, imperceptible to the senses, and of which witches alone are capable, by reason of the supernatural force at their disposal, and in second place the sense verifiable in the natural world. They are alike, but without being identical: and in the affective complex which is created as soon as the primitive man believes himself in the presence of an act of witchcraft, it is the first which is by far the most important and, as a result, the most certain. Thus, for the primitive mentality, far from there being there an incompatibility between two homogeneous facts, there is a correspondence, a figuration by the natural phenomenon of the action of supernatural cause.

Thus, I was wrong to seek something specifically logical to explain the above facts. It is not correct that Maliki does not see an incompatibility which seems evident to us and which he refuses to envisage. If he takes an attitude different from ours, it is because, for him, mystical experiences of an objectivity and certainty equal to those of ordinary experience are mingled in his daily experience, particularly when it is a matter of witchcraft. Now in the domain of mystical experience everything is possible, nothing is excluded, as (it is) in the domain of propositions bearing on ordinary experience, subject to rules if not to necessity. And whatever is positive in my idea of the prelogical character arises from the mystical character. The point is to show how.

June 24th, 1938.

Notebook III
June–August 1938

Not to confuse facts which are different and for which a common explanation could not serve. For instance, the Maliki case and that of Issifou.

1. Maliki seems at first incapable of grasping that he is asserting two incompatible things and that it is contradictory to say that both are true. If his daughter has been kidnapped, she is not dead in her hut; if it is correct that she is dead in her hut, she has not been kidnapped. If her body has been placed in the earth, she has not been cooked and eaten by the witches; if it is true that she has been cooked and eaten, it cannot be that her father has buried her body intact. Is Maliki incapable of understanding this *entweder-oder*? It would then be necessary to explain what causes this incapacity in him; and to ask, as I have done, if the logical requirements of his mind are not less than those of ours.

A more careful examination of the behaviour and words of Maliki (as far as we can accept that we have his own words, for they have to be taken as the interpreter gives them to us) shows that the question is badly asked or rather unaskable. Maliki is not incapable of seeing that between two incompatible claims it is necessary to choose, and that in the case of *entweder-oder* one of the claims excludes the other. Because there is incompatibility *for us* but not *for him*. It is true that his daughter is dead in her hut; he has seen her expire and grow cold. But that does not preclude her being the victim of a spiritual abduction; her soul, her life force has been taken away from her by the witches, and it is precisely this which caused her death. It is true that he himself has buried his daughter, and he indicates her grave from which her body is retrieved. But this does not rule it out that witches

45

have eaten her in their own way, a way which is invisible—
spiritual cannibalism.

Consequently we have no reason to suppose in Maliki, in this
circumstance, something specifically different from the logical
point of view from what occurs in us. It is enough to know that
the mystical beliefs and experiences common to his group explain
his words and deeds. Once given their ideas on sickness, on the
abnormality of death, on the power and malefices of witches, and
the rest follows. Maliki is consistent with himself, and finds that
it is the white man who is incapable of understanding. The Issifou
case is different. It does not involve an unperceived incompatibility between two claims, both of which the native nevertheless
accepts. The native simply does not choose between the many
ways in which a thing happened, and this attitude leads one to
think that for him they are equally true. Kanfory wanted Issifou's
death, and the latter succumbed in a very short time to a snake
bite. So rapid a death is more than suspect. There is witchcraft
at the bottom of it. Mystical inquiry, that is to say divination,
detection of the witch, who is Kanfory. No doubt in the group.

Now, was the snake an animal under the witch's orders, or was
Kanfory disguised as a snake in order to kill his victim? Impossible
to obtain a clear and satisfactory answer on this point. People
say one thing or the other, or sometimes one thing and sometimes
the other. If one presses them, if one points out to them that
it is not the same thing, they are evasive and the confusion
persists.

Do we have to say that they are incapable of seeing that if one
admits the truth of one of these hypotheses then it is necessary to
deny the other? In which case there would be a sort of logical
deficiency in them, as in the case where they do not perceive the
incompatibility of two mutually exclusive claims (a badly interpreted case, however, as we have just seen, the incompatibility
not being real for the native)?—Here again, looking at it close to
there is no place to introduce logical considerations. We say that
Issifou has been killed either by a snake under Kanfory's orders,
or by Kanfory himself who turned himself into a snake: in our
eyes there are two different explanations here of the action
executed by Kanfory. We distinguish them without difficulty,
because we represent both of them to ourselves clearly.

But the natives do not distinguish between them, because they do not think they have the means to do so. It is a matter of a witch's action: the latter proceeds *after the way of witches*, and ordinary people are unable to explain what he does. He has the choice of means: which does he choose? He alone knows. In fact, these means are of equal value; by one or other the end is equally attained. Let us not forget that the complex which is then produced in the natives is above all affective. What arouses them is the power of the witch who achieves his goals. What is important is to discover him, and to get rid of him.

Évian: June 25th, 1938.

FINAL RENUNCIATION OF THE PRELOGICAL CHARACTER

A closer examination has thus led me to a better interpretation of the facts collected in the accounts from French West Africa. I am more preoccupied to verify the preconceived idea of a difference, from the logical point of view, between the mental attitude of natives, in certain circumstances, and our own. As to the 'prelogical' character of the primitive mentality, I have already watered my wine for twenty-five years: the results which I have just reached concerning these facts make this development final, by making me abandon a badly founded hypothesis, at all events, in cases of this type.

Why had I conceived it, and why does nothing remain of it today?

Two reasons had made it more than plausible to me. 1. It seemed to me evident that at certain moments these minds followed paths that we do not take, and reciprocally, that they had extreme difficulty in following ours. This appeared to me to give proof of mental habits different from ours—habits which it was first important to describe well and the formation of which had therefore to be sought, as far as possible, together with their psychological and social origins.—2. I was guided by a need for symmetry. Our psychology and our logic have constituted, since antiquity, a body of problems concerning mental functions, and systems of solutions answering (more or less) these problems. Seeing that neither the description of these functions nor the solutions supplied for the problems concerning them could be used just as they are for the mental functions of primitive men,

I thought to seek 'what corresponded to them' in the case of primitive mentality. Which was, in short, a sort of extension of the far more radical hypothesis with which I started when I asked myself whether societies of different structure had not also, *ipso facto*, specifically different logics (for example, the idea of a peculiarly Chinese logic distinct from western logics).—I had quickly renounced this hypothesis which was at one and the same time simplistic and rather crude. But, when, in *How Natives Think*, I tried to establish that the primitive mentality differs from ours by its 'prelogical' character (as by its mystical character), it was possible to recognize there, in an already attenuated but basically similar form, this hypothesis which I afterwards felt to be without sufficient foundation.

From the point at which I am now, after what has been established in Volumes V and VI, it is necessary to abandon openly an arbitrary and artificial parallelism, which in wanting to find what in the primitive mentality 'corresponds' to one or another of our mental functions, raises pseudo-problems for which it is unimportant whether we find the answer or not. Consequently it would not be a matter simply of improving a good part of *How Natives Think* so as to make an edition corrected and completed by what I have been able to learn since 1910, but still maintaining the initial plan and assumptions (*Voraussetzungen*). It would be a matter of repeating the study of the facts to which I had believed it useful to apply that hypothesis, of making a fresh start.

In short, instead of *making* the facts *speak*, as I ventured to do in *How Natives Think*, convinced as I was in advance of what they were going to say and that they would make manifest the prelogical character of that mentality, instead of remaining attached to the essential of this very badly received hypothesis, and which seemed even to me more and more doubtful when I merely spoke of logical needs less exacting than ours, of mental habits different from ours, to have the scientific prudence *to let them speak*, and to presuppose nothing which might prevent one from seeing them as they are.

Therefore the first step will be to determine whether, in these facts, there is something specifically strange to our mental habits without imagining beforehand that the difference is of a logical nature. Can we establish it in connection with facts such as those of Maliki, of statements such as those in the business in the out-skirts of Conakry, etc.? The discussion summarized above shows clearly that we can manage to make these facts, in appearance incomprehensible and amazing, intelligible without having to call on any hypothesis analogous to those which I have slowly aban-doned. But that is only the negative aspect of what seems to me to be gained in rendering these facts intelligible. The positive aspect would be to reflect on what conditions they become so. Perhaps, in determining these conditions with all possible precautions, and without prejudging anything that cannot be checked, we will find a way of studying in a positive fashion the mental con-sequences of the mystical orientation of these societies.

Évian: June 27th, 1938.

QUESTION OF METHOD

Two points seem established and allow me to be a little closer to the truth than I was twenty years ago. 1. The logical structure of the mind is the same in all known human societies, just as they all have a language, customs and institutions; accordingly, to speak no longer of the 'prelogical' character and to say explicitly why I renounce this term and everything which it seems to imply; 2. to retain nevertheless the numerous and undeniable facts from which it is evident that the primitive mentality accepts, without flinching in the least degree, incompatibilities (I used to say 'contradictions' which has the air of implying some logical conditions which in reality do not exist) which catch our eye and which we do not understand how a sane mind can admit for a moment.

There is a difference between the primitive mentality and ours: not only that of the cultured, scientific man with a critical mind, but also that of the average man (save in exceptional circum-stances where, without thinking, he resumes the characteristic attitude of primitive men). Our problem, or at least one of our principal problems, will be to seek whence arises this amazing indifference to the most obvious and flagrant incompatibilities. If we succeed in determining the reasons we will see straightaway, or by almost direct inference, how the human mind has little by little, adopted another attitude, other habits, and also the main features of the transition from the primitive mentality to ours, at least on this important point.

An initial remark which may be useful: the indifference to incompatibility appears closely linked to the lack of curiosity about the question of knowing how improbable, absurd, and, according to us, impossible events occur. This indifference to 'how' is perhaps no more than another aspect of the indifference to incompatibility. Examples: the affair of Fatoumata; how has the child been eaten? The affair of Conakry: how were the five witches who, from the top of the rock, saw the crocodile attack Noussa, in the crocodile at the same time? To question the black men on the above is useless; they never ask themselves the question, and have no reply to it. But this means, in fact, that they do not understand its terms. If the question which seems so natural to us does not arise in their minds, if the terms of it are strange to them, there is reason for it. It is that their mind is preoccupied by something else. This is what it is necessary to seek first.

Bagatelle: July 14th, 1938.

BIMORPHISM OF A GUARDIAN SPIRIT

The account of the female shaman of the Oregon (Drucker, 280) throws a little light on the way in which primitive men represent to themselves individuals who are simultaneously humans and animals, for example the spirits who are the guardians of the North American shamans and who teach them their songs and procure them their powers. The above mentioned shaman has the customary number of guardian spirits: five who make their apperance successively in dreams: bear, yellow hammer, otter, etc. . . . They generally reveal themselves in human form and speak to her. The bear in particular appears as a man yet saying that he is a spirit, and reveals what he is ready to do in order that the woman may become 'a big doctor' and the conditions which she, on her side, must fulfil. But at another time he appears not in human form but as a bear; 'he had his fur'. The woman adds: 'He was no less a spirit.' He understands what she says to him.

It indeed seems for her that the essential thing is that it is a matter of an individual belonging to the supernatural (spirit) and as such disposing of supernatural forces which are those of a Bear spirit. That he appears as man or as a bear is of no importance (the form is only an accident, or clothing). He is both and shows himself sometimes as one and sometimes as the other.

Bois de Boulogne: July 29th [sic], 1938.

IMPOSSIBLE AND UNREALIZABLE FROM THE POINT OF VIEW
OF THE PRIMITIVE MENTALITY

Useless, certainly, to ask such questions of the natives, and if they replied one would be no further forward. But might we perhaps find in their utterances some indication of the way to take?

When, in the interrogations from French West Africa, the white man, intellectually scandalized by what the witnesses and the accused seem to admit with serenity—which seems to him absurd—tries to make them perceive the enormous incompatibilities, and presses them to say, for example, how the five witches of Conakry can at the same time see the crocodile on the beach from the top of the rock and be in the skin of the crocodile, they reply: 'It is the way of witches', just as Maliki, pressed to say how his daughter's body can have been stolen and eaten by the witches and nevertheless be found intact where he buried her, replies 'witches have every power'. The same reply is repeated regularly. It means: what you consider as impossible is so for ordinary people but not so for the witch; for him nothing is impossible. This answer, while fully satisfying for the native is not so for us. Why this difference? If we succeed in determining precisely the cause, we will have taken the first step. Now, it seems that once again we may have been fooled by implications of our vocabulary, and that, without taking care, we may make use of words which the primitive man does not employ or at least not in the sense which we do.

You accept, says the white man, something absurd and impossible.—Nothing, maintains he, is impossible for the witch.

But has 'impossible' the same sense for the interlocutors? For us it means 'not being able to be realized, because incompatible with the general conditions of experience which cannot be put in doubt, that is to say suspended in reality'. But the primitive man does not care about general conditions of experience outside which nothing can be real for us. Thus he will never say impossible, nor absurd (perhaps he has no term to express this idea, which sustains a minimum of logical reflection). In ordinary life, when it is not a question of witchcraft or of supernatural action, he rejects, as we do, what is absurd, but as it were instinctively and as M. Jourdain does with prose. If it is a matter of facts of the sort cited above, where supernatural forces are found involved, then he will not say: for the witch nothing is impossible, but rather: for him nothing is unfeasible. There is no task which he cannot accomplish, no obstacle which he does not surmount, no goal which he cannot attain. And this is indeed what is at the back of his mind when he says: 'Witches have every power.' They take their stand exclusively from the point of view of the result to be obtained, and do not preoccupy themselves at all with conditions of possibility for this result. They do not even think about it. Since the witch has every power, he can do even the absurd. Primitive man does not make this reflection, which is as far as possible from the ordinary activity of his mind, and as we have said he doubtless has not separated out the idea of the absurd.

If he had a feeling of it, he would not draw the same conclusion as we do from our idea of the absurd. For us, something which is clearly absurd is *ipso facto* impossible, and cannot be real. For the primitive man absurdity can be only relative, and does not entail the impossibility of existence, because the witch, being all-powerful, can accordingly also do the absurd. That is to say, as one has seen earlier, from the point of view of the action of the power (which is that of primitive man if he takes no other stand) impossible (absurd) can mean only 'unfeasible'. Now what characterizes the witch is precisely that for him there is no limit to what he can do. Consequently, when the white man explains to him that it cannot be that a body is at one and the same time eaten and intact, that some people are simultaneously on a rock and in a crocodile a hundred metres from the rock, this reasoning has no effect on him. In order that it might have, it would be necessary for the primitive man to have the sense of a limit to the possible in the surrounding reality. This sense is entirely lacking in him, once the affective category of the supernatural is at work.

Let us express that in the terms which we have used in Volumes

V and VI. In our thought, the conditions of the possibility of experience are universally valid for every experience, past and to come; what does not satisfy them cannot have been real nor ever become so. In the primitive man's world-view (*Weltanschauung*) the conditions of the possibility of experience such as we conceive them and feel them are valid only for ordinary experience; the mystical experience, the extraordinary experience is not subject to them: it is actually by this that it is characterized while remaining an experience. Proof: the mythical period and all the prodigies (which for us are inconceivable and fantastic) of which the myths are full. Proof: the mystical experiences which constantly occur and of which the above facts about witches form part.

July 16th, 1938.

Consequently if one asks: how can they accept without difficulty incompatibilities which according to us are enormous and more than obvious? The reply is: their mind is oriented in a different way from ours, and the fact that the mystical experience has for them at least as much objective value as the other experience helps to explain that manifest impossibilities for us may not be so for them.

In what concerns ordinary experience, they interpret and utilize rather as we do. The above question arises only with reference to mystical experience (it is this which is concerned in matters of witchcraft and other analogous cases). Now here two important considerations arise.

1. The cognitive point of view is entirely secondary to, subordinate to, and hidden by the emotions which are inseparable from the presence and action of supernatural forces. What, at this moment, occupies the consciousness of primitive man is the affective category of the supernatural. Before all he is preoccupied by the power of the supernatural forces; fear, respect and hope arise and demand recognition, more especially as he is impressed not simply by what they have just done, by what they are engaged in doing (sickness, persistent drought, etc.) but because of what they are going to do presently, without him having the means of knowing exactly what it will be and of warding it off—divination, auguries, etc., serve without doubt, but they do not suffice to give security.

This lively sensation *sui generis* of anxious disquiet expresses itself exactly through the belief in the witch's unlimited power, for example this power is such that for him there is nothing unfeasible, nothing unrealizable. The principally affective character of this complex makes complete, even rudimentary, analysis of this power impossible, and it does not allow there to be introduced into their mind a starting point for the attempt to take account of what this power is, and the way in which it attains its goals. It is there, it acts, and its aim is reached, or it will be after the delay that it fixes. In the very idea of this supernatural power is included [the consequence] that the result sought by it cannot but be obtained. (Show what remains of it, modified and transformed by civilizations and religions, in divine omnipotence. What characterizes it is the absence of any condition conceivable for the actual realization of its effects. It wishes, and its will is already done. Between it and its effects there is nothing. It is efficacious *per se*). We are thus led to the second consideration. The incompatibilities which primitive men accept without hesitation, we reject as impossible. However great may be the power of the witch, he cannot make the impossible become possible. There is nothing unfeasible for him, and that's that—nevertheless what he does must be feasible in itself. If the thing were such that it could not be realized, the power of the supernatural force, however immense one supposes or feels it to be, would have found its limit. Is there anything simpler and more obvious than that? How would a human mind, as little cultured, as little reflective as one might imagine it, not feel that, short of losing the feeling of its own activity, of its own reality?

It is indeed for this reason that, seeing primitive men accept as objectively real certain mystical experiences which according to us could only be fantastic and fabulous (stories, myths, etc.) and maintain that witches can do everything, without exception of any sort, without excluding the absurd and the obviously impossible, one is tempted to find an explanation in the convenient hypothesis that there is a difference from the logical point of view between the use which they make of their faculties and that which we do.

Bagatelle: July 17th, 1938.

In any case, if the hypothesis ought not to be rejected entirely I have convinced myself little by little that it cannot be retained under the rather simple and crude form which I proposed in 1910. I no longer speak of a prelogical character of the primitive mentality, even when clarifying the misunderstandings which this term has occasioned. From the strictly logical point of view no essential difference has been established between the primitive mentality and ours. In everything that touches on ordinary, everyday experience, transactions of all sorts, political and economic life, counting, etc., they behave in a way which involves the same usage of their faculties as we make of ours.

Where the question is complicated is where it is a matter of mystical experience—and it ought not to be forgotten, as has been shown in Volume VI, that the two experiences rarely present themselves separately from one another; on the contrary they are constantly entangled, intertwined in the life of primitive man who has only the idea of one experience in which both are included (subject to the emotion *sui generis* caused by the contact of the supernatural). How far does the difference which results from the primitive mentality's mystical orientation extend? What consequences are entailed by their faith in the mystical experience? Is there a logical repercussion?

July 17th, 1938.

EINSTEIN'S REFLECTION

Before entering into an examination of this question, a reflection on what I have just found in a recent article by Einstein *Zeitschrift für freie deutsche Forschung*, Paris, 1938, I, pp. 6–7):

'That the totality of cognitive experiences is of such a nature that it can be ordered by thought (working with concepts—creation and application of certain functional links between these as well as the attribution of these cognitive experiences to the concepts) is a fact at which we can only marvel but which we will never comprehend. One can say: the eternally incomprehensible thing about the world is that it is comprehensible. That it would be absurd to postulate an entirely incomprehensible universe is one of Immanuel Kant's great insights.'

F

Einstein here makes allusion to an epistemological problem (the subject of the article is *Physik und Realität*) which seems to have nothing in common with the one before us. Nevertheless his reflection, so profound, bears also indirectly on it. For, if we compare the mythical world with the world of ordinary experience such as philosophical and scientific endeavour has ordered it since antiquity, we will see that if the latter is comprehensible (*begreiflich*), the former is not, or at least is far from being so to the same degree.

Now, before the unintelligibility, at least relative of the mystical world, where the most extraordinary and inexplicable transformations occur, where the irregularity of phenomena appears as natural as their regularity, our mind experiences discomfort, confusion and perplexity: what is a world which is not rational and intelligible? And it gets out of it by saying: it is a world which is not real (imaginary, arbitrary, fabulous, like fairy stories). (Einstein says also that a world which would not be comprehensible (*begreiflich*) is senseless (*sinnlos*) and could not be real.) It is in our thought that the world of ordinary experience appears intelligible. For primitive men who do not reflect in this way, it is enough for them that it is generally regular and barely disappoints their expectation. [The preceding sentence is dated November 3rd, 1938].

But the philosopher can be tempted (and history shows that he has been and that he has usually succumbed to the temptation) to consider this rationality of the world which our science establishes and verifies, as reasonable in itself, as carrying in itself the reason of its legitimacy—this is what happens in a large number of metaphysical systems. It is here that Einstein's thought makes us reflect on ourselves. For he shows that this intelligibility of the sensible world, ordered and ruled by science, is itself for ever unintelligible. It is a fact which imposes itself on us, and Kant has shown that it is the condition of the reality of this existing world. But, at the same time, if it is a fact, and a fact which we cannot hope to explain, to render intelligible; is not consequently an absolute, something given or posed *a priori*, an indispensable assumption (*Voraussetzung*), and that gives us an indication, or at very least a valuable warning with regard to the special problem which we have to examine. For we can see it henceforth from the following angle:

Compared with the rational world of our sciences the mythical world is unintelligible, imaginary, and cannot be real: How does it happen that totally irrational as it is, with its impossibilities and absurdities, the primitive mentality takes it genuinely as real? In seeking the answer to this question, we know that the intelligibility of the rational world is itself unintelligible. Might there not be here simply a difference of degree? A transference of the unintelligibility of the detail to the world given in its totality?

July 18th, 1938.

AGREEMENT WITH LEENHARDT

The rereading of Leenhardt's manuscript on 'The religion of present-day primitive men' comes opportunely to prevent me from sliding too far down the slope where I now find myself. He does not treat of the question posed above, but gives an indication and even expressly says in what way we would resolve it. He does not doubt that primitive men's mental habits differ from ours (at least as soon as mystical experience is involved, as soon as it is a matter of religion, or what corresponds to it among primitive men, myths, traditional beliefs, in a word what we call supernatural and which, for them, is more or less distinguished from nature, but is above all not separated from it). He goes so far as to say that there the principle of contradiction is held in check and so far as to use the word 'prelogical'.

In order to avoid the misunderstandings which have brought me so much trouble, I will not resume the position which Leenhardt adopts here, and on the contrary I will insist on what I have put right. Once more I will affirm that the logical structure of the mind is the same for all men, and that as a consequence 'primitive men' reject contradiction, just as we do, when they perceive it. But at the same time, I will say, still in agreement with Leenhardt, that in the immense domain of the supernatural they do not generally perceive it and thus are not shocked by it. Cite here some very profound formulae from his chapter on myths, which I could do in any case and which is all the more legitimate since Leenhardt consciously takes his inspiration from my *Primitive Mentality* and expressly says so himself (for example, what relates to mythical time which is not defined by succession;

myths do not unfold in time; on the contrary, it is time which is
in the myth, etc.).

2. I am able to go a little further with Leenhardt. Mythical
thought, he says (as I had indicated in *How Natives Think* but
with less precision, because I was not speaking of mythical
thought but only of the primitive mentality in general), is not
conceptual. It only juxtaposes, it does not classify. This is where
my current thoughts again lead. As this thought does not classify,
there are no—or very few—inclusions and exclusions, and as a
consequence the incompatibilities and contradictions which are
insupportable for us do not present themselves to them. Thus it is
not necessary to say that they tolerate them. They have neither
to tolerate nor to reject them: they do not exist for them.
Leenhardt shows very well how from this point of view the fluidity
of the mythical world is explained, and the incoherence and
uncoordination of the events which take place in that world; and
as I still do, he insists on the part of the emotional element
(*affective* category of the supernatural).

Thus we draw near the solution sought. From the point of
view of thought, what is the consequence of the mystical character
essential to the primitive mentality, of the importance which the
mystical experience has for them, in short of the action of the
affective category of the supernatural?—This thought is naturally
mythical, that is to say extra-temporal and non-conceptual.

Direct consequence: between the representations, the scenes
which occupy the consciousness by turns, there cannot be contradiction. But then, do we say, there is confusion, disorder? Is this
compatible with a truly human thought?—Disorder implies an
order more or less rational or even artificial. But *order* means
classification, subordination, that is to say something very different
from the juxtaposition which characterizes this mythical thought:
the mythical world which is the projection of it, the myths which
are the expression or mirror of it. Likewise confusion implies
distinction; clear distinction, again, implies concepts. Accordingly
let us not say confusion, but let us recognize participation here.

Bois de Boulogne: July 20th, 1938.

CONCEPT: LOGICAL GENERALITY
PARTICIPATION: AFFECTIVE GENERALITY

In support of this last consideration, cite an excellent passage
from Leenhardt (manuscript 'Religion of present-day primitive
men') which brings out the difference between the thought of
these primitive men in so far as it is not conceptual, and ours in its
daily and usual form. Leenhardt shows the participations which
coexist at a given moment in the consciousness of a Kanaka; with
the ancestors, totems, earth, rocks, rivers, mountains, the living
and the dead of his clan, etc. No conception of an order, but
feeling of assemblages, of solidarities, or of common participations
(ancestors, totems, configuration of the earth, animals and vege-
tables, etc.). Each of these participations is felt qualitatively; they
neither conflict nor order themselves; they juxtapose themselves
in him as they do in other members of the group. But from their
simple enumeration and from their affective character it is evident
that they cannot give birth to an ordinary and hierarchical view
of the things in which the Kanaka feels himself to participate.
Each among them is *separate*. As I said in Volume IV, when I
introduced the affective category of the supernatural, what strikes
one at once when one studies it is that if one can truly call it a
category, that is to say discern in it an element of generality, this
generality consists of this, that the subject's emotion through
contact with the supernatural is always the same. Recognized
immediately, like a perceptible datum of sight, smell, etc., which
is *sui generis*, it is indeed revealing, but revealing only of itself,
in the presence and in the action of a supernatural force, but
one cannot say it is of knowledge. Put differently, it is not
accompanied by a concept. Each participation is individual, the
general element is of an affective order.

Consequence, where the essential difference between the concept and the participation becomes apparent. Participation has
reality only in so far as it is felt by an individual (even if similar
participations occur at the same moment among various members
of the group, who have, for example, a single mystical experience).
It is thus an event which occurs *hic et nunc*, localized in space
and time, or better said which has its own space and time. Whence
it follows, as again says Leenhardt, that in the mythical world

there are no contradictions, but only contrasts; events either come to terms with each other or disagree more or less strongly with each other; in so far as they are felt in their own space and time they clearly cannot exclude one another. Hence the impression of chaos or confusion often produced by the myths whose unordered content seems absurd, although it is not since in the domain of the supernatural or of participation the distinction between what is absurd and what is acceptable to understanding does not apply. But we find there juxtapositions, repetitions, imitations, even more or less regular series.

On the contrary, concepts are not events. They appear as products of the mind's activity which seeks to introduce an order into the variegated mass of sense-data, and which there finds a double importance: from the point of view of action to make it more prompt and sure of itself, from the point of view of the mind itself which enjoys the rationality perceived in nature and according to its propensities. (Introduce here what I have to say that is new about abstraction, classification, schemata, induction, deduction, etc.) In these domains, which are alien to participation and where it only finds its place with difficulty, the general element is of the highest importance and the generality which, in the domain of participations, belongs only to the affective character of the participations which, like events, are always particular belongs on the contrary in essence to the concept, the particular appearing only when an object is subsumed in an actual or imagined experience.

Bois de Boulogne: July 28th, 1938.

NO 'LAW' OF PARTICIPATION

In *How Natives Think* it seems that participation had been suggested to me by the difficulty of explaining the way in which the (collective) representations of the primitive mentality are linked to one another. Not being able to explain certain connections through steps of thought obeying the laws of logic, I imagined I had to have recourse to a *law of participation*.

But today I would no longer take this position, and for many reasons. I know a much larger number of facts and I analyse them better than thirty years ago. In the first place, as was pointed out to me a long time ago, it is legitimate to speak of participation and I have given some incontestable examples of it (appurtenances, symbols, relation of the individual to the social group, etc.); it is not so legitimate to speak of a *law* of participation, a law which, as I myself immediately acknowledge, I cannot formulate exactly, or even in an approximately satisfactory way. What exists is the *fact* (not the law) that 'primitive man' very often has the feeling of participation between himself and such and such surrounding things or objects, of nature or of the supernatural, with which he is in or enters into contact, and that no less frequently he imagines similar participations between these things and objects (superabundant proofs in myths).

In the second place, it is not in the connections of representations that the existence of participations is most clearly manifested. The idea of representations, sorts of entities separated or at least always separable that one must find a satisfactory means for the mind to connect (say something about *Gestalt psychology*), forms part of an assemblage of outdated psychological and logical conceptions derived evidently from the associationist school and its English and French predecessors of the eighteenth and nineteenth centuries. Their way of posing problems gives way before a more exact knowledge of the facts, and for the most part they debated only pseudo-problems. They rely on assumptions (*Voraussetzungen*) which themselves are unfounded. One of the best established results in my researches concludes in favour of the definite abandonment of these problems and of the collection of ideas that gave rise to them. Thus, no longer to speculate on representations and on their 'connections'; thus no longer to make participation intervene in the solution of problems which are only pseudo-problems. In consequence, take the examples of participation given in *How Natives Think* (and in the following volumes) and give a more exact analysis of them.

Bois de Boulogne: July 27th, 1938.

The impression which is borne out, following what I have set forth in Volumes V and VI, following the records of French West Africa, and the article for the 'Nouvelle Revue Française' can be summarized thus: I was wrong, in *How Natives Think*, in wishing to define a character peculiar to the primitive mentality as far as logic is concerned, in believing that the facts, in certain cases, showed this mentality to be insensitive or at least more indifferent than ours to contradiction. Examined without prejudice, the facts say nothing at all, and participation itself involves, in essence, nothing incompatible with the principle of contradiction. That it may be refractory to analysis is not in doubt, and I will have to discover the reasons for it—but it does not follow that it is unacceptable to a mind which thinks logically. A huge problem, fundamental to the work which occupies me at the moment and to which it will be necessary to settle down soon. Today I would merely wish to note with some precision the impression that I spoke about just now.

1. (What I had not discerned at the period of *How Natives Think*) these minds do not differ from ours from the logical point of view, not only in their structure but also in the manifestations of their activity. (Practical matters, techniques, language, counting, etc.)

Thus they no more support a formal contradiction than we do. They reject, as we do, through a sort of mental reflex, what is *logically* impossible, absurd in the strict sense of the word.

2. It is completely different with the physically impossible. There is an infinity of such forms and cases which we reject with the same vigour, which in the eyes of the primitive mentality, can and even must be accepted as real. The contrast appears, for example, when it is a matter of myths, stories and legends. We have the greatest difficulty in believing that these histories are taken by primitive men in all seriousness for something which has really happened and still happens, that they are true, in the full sense of the word, and that the mythical world, with its own time and its fluidity, is a world no less objective than that of ordinary experience. Can we not go further than the establishment of this contrast (which has no logical foundation, as I thought at first it had), and seek the reasons for it?—I have said something about it, but in too vague and general a fashion, in the last chapter of *How Natives Think* when considering the evolution of the primitive mentality in its main features under the influence of technical progress. More is now necessary.

Bagatelle: July 28th, 1938.

HOW MYTHS ARE TRUE STORIES

I have always felt that there is something insufficiently clear in the way in which I represent the mythical world, and the world where mystical experience enters, which it reveals, and the relations between these two worlds. Do they form only one, or are they distinct? And if the latter, in what way are they distinguished? Questions of great importance, which as soon as they arise I cannot but study.

Perhaps I might start by defining more precisely a formula of which I made use in Volumes V and VI, where I often had the occasion to say that for primitive men myths are stories of what has taken place, *true* stories, but without having asked myself what exactly is the meaning of the word *true* here. I have taken as agreed that 'true' (concerning mythical or legendary stories) means 'what has really happened' as the history of Napoleon or Caesar is a true story, that of Pantagruel or Don Quixote is not. We do not see another sense in which a story may be said to be true or not true; there are not two ways for an event, an act, a thing to be objectively real.

Now this position, which to us seems indisputable, is not however that of the primitive mentality. Just as its experience is wider than ours—ordinary experience and mystical experience—so also its 'reality' is not univocal: that is to say events and beings can be real for it which are not for us, and some stories can be true which we cannot accept as such. Only just as the mystical experience, while being truly an experience, has characteristics which distinguish it from the other, so also myths and legends are true stories, but their 'truth' has characteristics which distinguish it from that of the events of everyday life.

In other words, myths are histories which have truly happened but which have taken place in a time, in a space, and in a world which is not identical with the time, space and world of the present, and which, though distinct if not separate, is no less 'real'. Therefore, to say that these are true stories is not to assimilate them purely and simply to what has happened in the tribe yesterday and today. It is a reality which is felt at one and the same time as beyond doubt and as having something peculiar to it which characterizes it directly.

Le Minihic: August 4th, 1938.

Compare the above with what I said about myths in the last chapter of *How Natives Think*: that myths are the sacred history of 'primitive' societies. If this is so, the question of knowing whether they are true stories or not does not arise for them. The aspect with which they are passionately concerned is their sacred character (like that of our religious history). The latter, having its origin in the revelation, at the same time finds there the guarantee of its veracity, if need be: could there be an attitude more perfect, more unshakeable than that in the word of God?— *Mutatis mutandis*, one can say as much of myths. In this case again, the sacred, 'supernatural' character of myths implies, as a direct consequence, that nothing they recount is to be doubted. There is no question of it.—Therefore, they are true stories— revelations relative to an extratemporal period, full of individuals and events which belong to the supernatural but to which real nature is bound and from which it is inseparable.—And it is exactly those relations which they contain that attest to their sacred character and assure it an unrivalled authority, which can also be said of holy books.

Le Minihic: August 6th, 1938.

QUESTIONS OF VOCABULARY AND METHOD

Since *How Natives Think* I have explained a certain number of peculiarities of the primitive mentality by saying that it was not conceptual—and Leenhardt has declared me right and has followed me on this point. I believe it to be very important, as he does. It implies the special nature of abstraction, generalization, and classification in the mind of primitive men. What I have said about it is not wrong—but the negative part, the operations which the primitive mentality uses little or not at all—the easiest —is the only one I have stressed and have employed with some precision. In a new work on the mental activity of 'primitive men', it is indispensable that I try to study more thoroughly the positive part,—a study little elaborated until now, and rendered particularly difficult by the necessity either of employing the vocabulary of our philosophers and psychologists, a perpetual cause of misunderstanding and misinterpretation in the description and analysis of the facts since one cannot ask the reader to strip the words of their atmosphere and their universally accepted associations; or of forging a new vocabulary, the inconveniences and dangers of which would be perhaps still worse, for unless this vocabulary is entirely new, it asks of the reader a constant and excessive effort which tires him and discourages him; it recalls more or less closely the traditional terms to which a new sense is attributed, and there is no use in taking the greatest care in defining them, for confusions are inevitable, wrong meanings and misinterpretations occur, and also misunderstandings which the most energetic and express rectifications never suffice to dissipate.

To this problem I see no satisfactory solution, and I can only choose the least bad. The wise thing seems to be to avoid above all neologisms, and as far as possible the employment of usual words in an unaccustomed sense. If the work took on a dialectical form, there would be nothing much to hope for, and the verbal distinctions would not be able to prevent confusion; rather they would engender it. It is in the exactness of apprehending the facts before expressing them and putting them into words that there resides a possibility of safety; to feel and to understand the mental activity in question before forcing it into the frameworks with which our thought has rendered us so familiar that they appear to be necessary.

In the first place, is it the primitive mentality considered in its totality, *in globo*, which is not conceptual? Or is it only when it operates in the domain of ordinary experience, or in that of mystical experience? *How Natives Think* is not explicit on this point: I speak there only of 'collective' representations, their connections and pre-connections, and collective, describe there, but only roughly, the domain which I will call the mystical experience. However, the facts cited and analysed in the first part, and also in the second part where I treat of languages and numeration among 'primitive men', show that I make no distinction between the two domains. Moreover, as I have shown in Volume VI, primitive men themselves do not separate them though distinguish them: they constitute together only a single experience; and the surrounding world with the mythical world constitutes for them a single rather than a double reality.

That granted, it is interesting to note that, in the chapters which treat of concepts, abstractions, etc., and of languages, it is a question only of the operations of the primitive mentality in so far as it acts upon the data of ordinary experience (superabundance of names for sub-species and varieties, few general ideas, classifications not resting on analysis and abstraction, reflection of all this in the language, etc.).

From there a question which puts in more precise terms the general problem indicated just now: Am I still at the same point? In *How Natives Think* and the two following works, I was above all preoccupied with showing that, in its *daily activity*, the primitive mentality did not operate in the same way as ours: used memory more than reason whenever possible, had a certain aversion for discursive operations, abstraction, generalization, etc., and accumulated knowledge rather than organize that which it had acquired. This is moreover Leenhardt's thought when he says that this primitive mentality juxtaposes, and does not classify.

But in these characteristics peculiar to the primitive mentality acting upon experience I pointed out yet another thing of capital importance: what, at that moment, I called the law of participation, the role of which has become, in time, more and more important. Is there a relation between the function of this law and the characteristics peculiar to the primitive mentality which *How Natives Think* insists as differentiating it from ours? And is it not remarkable that whereas the facts concerning these characteristics belong almost entirely to the domain of ordinary experience, as soon as it is a question of participation the facts are borrowed from the domain of mystical experience? That which has the most struck readers, the Bororo-parrot duality, and most of the others are intelligible only as mystical experiences (communion of the social group with its totem, organic solidarity of individuals with their group, their clan, meaning of initiation ceremonies, etc.).

I therefore found myself led, already in *The Soul of the Primitive*, but especially beginning with *Primitives and the Supernatural* and still more in Volumes V and VI, to insist on what I have called the affective category of the supernatural, the apprehension of the mythical world, the specificity of the mystical experience which it is impossible to confuse with the other experience, although not separate from it. Participation is implied everywhere, and it is no longer a question of discursive operations, but of revelation and immediate apprehension. Meanwhile I have kept on speaking of category and generality. Why? That is what must be cleared up.

Le Minihic: August 7th, 1938.

Notebook IV
August 8th–August 18th, 1938

In the representations and beliefs of ordinary experience as well as mystical experience, participation occupies a more or less important place according to circumstances. I understand this much better today than when I spoke of it for the first time in 1910. I can therefore try, for the types of participation with which I am most occupied, to see what mental activity they imply, and how they are related to the operations of the mind which I studied in the first and second parts of *How Natives Think*.

Among the very instructive forms of participation on which I dwelt only later, I will retain appurtenances, bi- or multi-presence, and symbols, in order to combine them with participation between the individual and his group, between the group and its totem, between the group and the mythical ancestors, the earth, what lives off it and on it, etc. To study of what participation consists in these various cases, how it is felt, the complexes in which it presents itself, what, in these complexes, can be the part of abstraction (what sort of abstraction?) of 'patterns' or schemes, and that of the affective elements (analyse, if possible, the affective category of the supernatural when it is a matter of mystical experience).

Le Minihic: August 8th, 1938.

What I have said until now about participation is very little. Nevertheless it is one of the points which has most attracted and held attention, and which has been most generally accepted. Perhaps precisely because I limited myself to stating the facts, which are undeniable, and to showing that the behaviour of 'primitive men' in a large number of circumstances clearly

involved participations felt or represented by them: relations of
the individual and the group, of the group and the totem,
appurtenances and usages which are made of them: charms,
footsteps, remains of food, secretions, relations of the symbol and
that which it represents, etc., bi- and multi-presence. That primitive men act as if these participations were as real for them as
the relations objectively established between phenomena are for
us, for example between secondary causes and their effects, it is
not enough to say that primitive men believe it: their ways of
acting, their prohibitions and taboos are most often only explicable
through the participations of which they have to take account,
which they desire to establish or avoid, or turn to their profit
(symbolic actions, numerous examples in Volume VI).

All this can hardly be contested, and, in fact, it has not been.
Criticism had nothing to get hold of. The facts are clear, and are
to be found in all more or less primitive societies; their interpretation, namely that in 'primitive men' they involve the feeling or
representation of participations, is not in doubt. Perhaps it might
have been otherwise if I had proposed a theory. Perhaps also I
have been wiser in abstaining from doing so. To be honest, I did
not have one. Had I had a theory, it would probably have given
rise to objections (perhaps well founded ones) and what would
have gone against the theory would doubtless have gone also
against the description and analysis of the facts; so that what now
seems to have been gained would still be a subject of debate.
Therefore it has been more valuable perhaps that, until now, I
have confined myself, concerning participation, to the little that I
have said, more especially as I represent participation as 'refractory to analysis' by its nature and impossible to make intelligible:
an *a priori* condemnation of every explanatory theory since, if it
succeeds in making participation intelligible, it is therefore wrong
and destroys its object.

Le Minihic: August 10th, 1938.

Can I not try, ought I not now to try, to go a little further? On
condition, of course, that I do not take my stand from the point of
view of the theory of cognition (*Erkenntnissetheorie*), that I guard
against all dialectic, that I do not appeal to 'faculties' of the
mind or soul, etc., in brief on condition that I do not deviate

from the method followed until now, and which the results obtained have appeared to justify.

Therefore my research will bear on these facts: to give, when possible, a more precise account of the facts, and above all to develop the analysis without falling into abstract dialectic. And to which facts, from preference, to apply myself? In general they are of two sorts: beliefs in participations felt or represented (participation with the totemic ancestor, participation of the Naga with his leopard, etc. . . . and ways of acting or abstaining founded on participations felt or represented (sympathetic magic, symbolic actions of all sorts, etc. . . .). It seems that I ought to study both categories of facts, but that yet, in principle, symbolic actions are those which expose one less to errors of interpretation—less than beliefs, in any case.

Le Minihic: August 10th, 1938.

PARTICIPATION OF APPURTENANCES

Take a symbolic action the meaning of which for the natives who practise it is without ambiguity—for example, to strike a spear into the footprint of an enemy or animal who is out of range. They think that the wound made in the imprint strikes simultaneously the man or animal who left it. He is thus as vulnerable in this imprint as in the foot itself. We recognize here the same procedure as in a large number of cases of witchcraft (sympathetic magic, action on the remains of food, on hair, excrement, nails, clothes impregnated with sweat, etc. . . . , in short on the appurtenances). We interpret these procedures by the conviction, established among the natives, that the appurtenances *are* the individuals themselves; there is between them and their appurtenances a participation so that what affects the appurtenances affects simultaneously the individuals. The footprint is the foot itself; the foot, by virtue of the principle *pars pro toto* or of the participation of all the parts of the organism, *is* the animal or the man himself, as is his picture or his name. The native's action would have no sense if he were not persuaded of its efficacy, that is to say of participation.

Le Minihic: August 10th, 1938.

When we say that the native's action is suggested to him by a participation felt or represented between the footprint in the sand and the enemy or animal which is already far away, are we sure that this term expresses exactly his state of mind, and what makes him act thus? I do not know if primitive languages in general have a word for 'participation' in the sense in which we understand it, and I am inclined to think not: they hardly have the habit of reflecting on such subjects or on abstract ideas of this type. What participation in this case means for us is a 'sympathy' between the two individuals or objects which participate with one another. The animal in flight is a real thing—the pattern traced in the sand by its foot is another, not only distinct from the animal which exists without it, as it exists without the animal, but separated from it spatially by a greater or smaller distance (as a portrait of an Australian aborigine may be found in England, and yet an action exercised on this picture has its repercussion on the model who is 26,000 kilometres away). This distinction, this separation in point of fact, does not, we think, stop 'primitive man' representing to himself the action exercised on the one as being also exercised on the other, because, despite appearances and the distance, there is something in common between them which establishes a sympathy, in the etymological sense of the word. The footprint is not foreign to the animal since it is its foot which has left it; the photograph is not foreign to the Australian since it reproduces his features. In this way we explain a belief in which we do not share, and the ways of acting based on it. We do not accept those 'sympathies' which experience does not allow to be verified; we simply see that 'primitive men' act as if these sympathies were real.

But this way of understanding participation does not seem to correspond exactly to what it is among 'primitive men'. The study of appurtenances and that of symbols, of bi-presences, etc. . . . , shows that it is not a matter only of a 'sympathy' between distinct individuals or objects, but that participation, in a very large majority of cases, is felt as consubstantiality. The man and his appurtenances, for example his hair, saliva, footprint, etc. . . . , *are* one and the same thing, as are he and his name. The stone is not the domicile of the ancestor, of his spirit; it is the ancestor himself, petrified (Leenhardt, Melanesians, *Zeitschrift für Ethnologie*). Between the Naga and *his* leopard there is not only a sympathy which causes the reaction on the man of the action exercised on the leopard; there is not an identity (an abstract notion which they do not possess), but a concrete consubstantiality which our languages lack a word to express.

It is a matter of dual-units (Leopards-men, individual-appurtenances) of which we are able to form an approximate idea only by an effort of depriving this expression of its abstract nature—not at all constricting for us, familiar as we are with numbers expressed in language—but surely alien to 'primitive men's' states of consciousness. For them, duality-unity is not the synthesis or reunion of *one* thing with *another* thing, such that while being *two* they are yet only *one*. Paying no attention to the representation of one thing (the animal) and of another (the footprint in the sand) they have no need for an act of the mind which reunites them and fuses the two 'units' into a 'duality' which is a sort of superior unity. What is for us a duality-unity when we try to represent to ourselves what there is in their mind is simply a complex reality, felt *at one and the same time* as one and as two without this causing any difficulty. The photograph is felt as *being* the very person of whom it is the portrait; the footprint in the sand as *being* the very animal which has escaped; the leopard in the jungle as being the very Naga who lives in the neighbouring village. The ideas of 'one' and 'two' play no part here in 'primitive man's' thought.

This is what one must not lose sight of when, in order to explain the participations on which are founded so many of the practices in use among 'primitive men', we say that they are 'dual-units'. The expression can be accepted (and Leenhardt has accepted it) on condition that one does not forget that it is a translation, in our abstract language, for something very different and for which we do not have an appropriate term—of the feeling that the individual and his appurtenances, the animal and its tracks in the sand, the subject and his portrait, the Naga and his leopard *are*—although separated in space and distinct—consubstantial.

Le Minihic: August 11th, 1938.

WHY THERE IS NOT AN ADEQUATE VERBAL EXPRESSION

Two points to be elucidated, on which what I have said concerning participation is far from satisfactory.

1. The appurtenances *are* the individual: the leopard *is* the Naga; the stone *is* the petrified ancestor; the skull *is* the person who is dead, etc. . . . What meaning has the verb 'to be' for the 'primitive men' who are convinced of these participations? In many of their languages this verb does not exist in a form corresponding to the term 'to be' in ours. Those languages have recourse to other methods of expression. Even where a verb 'to be' does exist, is it used to express participation, that is to say that what is 'participated in' and what participates are reunited into only one, in such a way, for example, that the portrait or the footprint is the very man or animal? Perhaps there might be reason to consider separately the case of the symbol (representative identified with that which it represents, Leenhardt's case of the petrified ancestor) and that of pure participation (between the man and his appurtenances, between the Naga and his leopard, etc. . . .). In order to give an idea of what this relation represents in the eyes of the primitive mentality I have made use of the word 'consubstantiality'. But it is too abstract to give the desired enlightenment; it has no positive content here other than that of repeating under another form that the hair *is* the individual, that the portrait *is* the subject, that the leopard *is* the Naga, etc. . . . The obscurity of the verb 'to be' is not dissipated at all.

Perhaps the difficulty of finding a satisfactory expression arises from the fact that the primitive mentality does not express participation, since it does not feel the need to. All the participations cited are *felt* by those whom they affect in various ways and from whom they provoke reactions, emotional and motory, most often in a way preordained by tradition. 'Primitive man' feels that the track is inseparable from the animal, the portrait from the subject, etc. . . . It is an immediate apprehension which is sufficient in itself, as a belief or an experience, and which does not at first present itself in the form of a proposition with a verb: the track *is* the animal; the portrait *is* the subject. If the 'primitive man' has to reply to a question which the white man asks him on

the subject of such and such a participation (Bororo-parrot), supposing that he understands what the white man wants to know,
how will he be able to answer? In the sentence which he will use,
the feeling of the participation will necessarily be changed in
being verbally expressed—whether or not he employs the verb
'to be' there will be two representations and a perceived relation
expressed between the objects of these representations: identity,
consubstantiality, sympathy, solidarity, duality-unity, etc. . . . It
is a translation of participation. One has passed from the level of
what is felt to the level of what is represented. In this passage the
essence of participation has escaped.

Now when above all the feeling is strong and intense, the
representation of the relationship is superfluous. It could be said
that it is included, potentially and to a high degree in the very
feeling of the participation. The aboriginal Australian woman
who believes herself lost because some of her hair is in the possession of another does not need to know in what sense her hair is
she herself. She has a *felt* certainty which in no degree depends on
the awareness, even instantaneous, of the relationship between
herself and her hair. *We* say that it is she herself.

Le Minihic: August 12th, 1938.

PARTICIPATION INDEPENDENT OF SPACE

We do not easily see how participation is established and how it
subsists despite a separation in space, which is sometimes considerable. Bi- or multi-presence causes us an uneasiness: the dead
Bantu petty king who *is* several lion cubs, who is reincarnated in
the son who is born to his own son, and yet who is at the same
time in his tomb and in the land of the dead—the Runga of
Junod who occupies three sepulchres: that where his body is
buried—that where his clothes, and his ornaments, which are
himself, have been thrown—and his house which is also treated
as an appurtenance. Facts of this type are innumerable, in regions
which are most distant from one another. To what extent can we
understand them? Are they truly participations?

In the cases of duality-unity, it seems that on this last point
there is no doubt. The 'consubstantiality' of the Naga and his
leopard is a beautiful example of participation. The Naga is also

and at the same time the leopard in the jungle. This leopard is also and at the same time the Naga in the village. The case of the Bantu petty king is of the same sort. To 'understand' them in the ordinary sense of the word is more than difficult, and the considerations above concerning the word 'to be' are again relevant here. We can only get round it by saying that participation is felt in accordance with traditional beliefs of which the difference from real experience tends towards zero.

The case of the Bantu who has three graves is a little different. Without doubt, this tri-presence also has as its reason participations, at very least so far as the tomb is concerned where his appurtenances have been placed, and his house. It is the participation between him and them which makes him *felt* to be present there, and hence it seems legitimate to place cases of this type together with the preceding ones. What disturbs us is the violence done to one of our mental habits. We take for granted, as going without saying, and having no need to be proved or even stated, that if a thing or an object is found at a given moment and in a certain place it is not found at the same moment in another place, distinct and sometimes very far from the first. We are the more firm in this affirmation in that it seems more or less consciously implied in the postulates of mathematics: if a point did not occupy a certain place, indivisible, and one only, geometry would not be possible. Now although our geometry, as a science, works with the abstract, it has nevertheless an infinity of concrete applications, and this is probably one of the reasons that bi-presence and other participations cited above do not appear acceptable to us. My first attitude, before reflection, was even to judge them to be contradictory, which strictly speaking they are not. There is no contradiction properly so called in maintaining at the same time that 'A' is present in a certain place and that he is also in another place. Religions, in general, see this as no difficulty for their gods (recall also the Lengua Indian in Grubb).

Nevertheless if the bi- or multi-presence is not contradictory, it does appear to us practically unthinkable, and as it is closely linked to participation this is one of the reasons why participation seems to us as 'unamenable to intelligibility'. How does it happen that the primitive mentality, on the contrary, accepts it without seeing anything to take it aback? The fact is certain: if we can account for it, we will have taken a step forward.

One might say to begin with that the primitive mentality is predisposed towards it, on the one hand because it is accustomed to see myths, in which cases of bi- and multi-presence are not rare, as true stories, and also through its mystical experiences, in particular the presence of the dead, with whom they feel convinced they are in contact, although at the same moment they may be in the Land of the Dead with the 'other members of the clan', dead like them. I have cited a good number of such facts.

On the other hand one must not lose sight of the fact that in these societies the solidarity of each individual with his group (family, sib, clan, phratry) is not felt or represented as it is in ours. In the latter, certainly, each individual feels himself solidary—up to a certain point— with his parents and children, with his fellow citizens, with different circles to which he belongs as a result of his occupations, interests, tastes, beliefs, etc. . . . But he has no less the conviction that his person is an individuality constituted in its own right, which has almost entire responsibility for his decisions and acts, and, on this score, is clearly separate from others, even from those who are closest to him. Not so in a clan of 'primitive men'. Doubtless the individual there has a clear awareness of his individuality in so far as in this awareness there echo, in the form of psychic phenomena, certain sensations, emotions, perceptions and images, which act on his organism or on his mind by means of language or reflection on what happens to him: his joys, sorrows, reactions, etc. . . . , and these are individual (although nearly always socialized, that is to say conforming to traditional patterns). But, that accepted, he is linked to other members of his group by a solidarity far tighter and more intimate than any in our societies, and which, as I have shown in *The 'Soul' of the Primitive*, is almost organic (interchangeable brothers, collective responsibility, etc. . . .).

Consequently the real person, the real individual, is the group (tribe, clan, family, etc. . . .). Those whom we call individuals are the members of it, in the biological sense of the term. In the complex of emotions and representations which we regard as their self, what predominates is the liaison of that self with the group of which it forms part (amply proved by preceding works: initiation, fear of being excluded from the clan after death, etc. . . .). That is to say that each feels himself—in so far as there is here an object of thought for him—represents himself to himself

as an element of everything social and organic to which he
belongs and in which he participates. Give to these terms their
full meaning. One might almost say that each individual is an
appurtenance of the clan, since what affects the clan *ipso facto*
affects him, and reciprocally, which is, as we have seen, the
essential characteristic of a participation.

Now as for the other members who, with him, compose this
totality, who are, like him, the constitutive elements of the clan,
who participate in it like him, he does not see them as united,
assembled, and inseparable like the members of a living body.
The members of the social body are separate and independent
from each other in space. They move and change place freely;
very often members of a single clan live in different villages, and
it happens that they may never see each other. And yet each of
them feels that he is what he is through his participation in the
common stock—not simply in the clan as it exists in the present,
but in the more or less recently deceased ancestors and in the
mythical ancestors, and in the totem of the group. Accordingly, in
the course of his own existence, each individual continually has
the experience of participation with individuals from whom he is
separated in space. Therefore he finds nothing strange in bi-
presence.

Le Minihic: August 13th, 1938.

PARTICIPATION OF THE INDIVIDUAL IN THE SOCIAL BODY

What precedes is not inexact, but most inadequate to help explain
what participation is, because it is too schematic, incomplete and
superficial. Despite myself, I am always led by epistemological
(*erkenntnistheoretisch*) preoccupations, and participation plays
for me the role of a guiding principle, like the principle of identity
or causality. Now nothing imposes or even justifies this parallelism, except some inveterate habits of the philosopher or psychologist, and doubtless also the naive need to follow the line of least
effort, of least resistance, by asking questions according to a
common model. But to carry on thus cannot give a truly
satisfactory result: it is in the impartial examination of the facts
that one must ask how the question may usefully be put, and to
place oneself at the point of view of the theory of knowledge is

equivalent to vitiating in advance what one will find to say about participation, since by its nature it is impossible to make it transparent and intelligible. If my earlier work has a positive content and a utilizable value, it is necessary consequently to disengage this content from the form under which it has just been presented.

The consciousness which 'primitive man' has of his individuality, we were saying, is enveloped in a complex where the predominant element is the feeling that the individual has of 'belonging' to a group which is the true individuality and of which he is simply an element, like the other members, in the true sense of the word, of the social body. This feeling is thus that of a participation. The consciousness which he has of himself is not the awareness of a person complete in himself, but of a person for whom the *raison d'être*, the essential conditions of existence, are found in the group of which he forms part, and without which he would not exist. This conviction is not formulated in express terms in the thoughts of 'primitive man'. He has neither the need for reflection nor the linguistic material which would be indispensable for that. But what we find in him, in all societies called primitive, is the feeling of this almost organic solidarity, which is expressed not through formulae but in a living manner through the institutions (family, clan, totemism, customs, religious beliefs, etc. . . .) which all rest on participations, of which that of the individual with the social body to which he feels himself to belong is the prototype and, as it were, the root.

Do we thus account for participation and the function which it constantly fulfils in the working of the primitive mentality?— Yes and no. Yes, because this feeling of 'belonging' to a whole of which the individual feels himself part, an element, seems indeed to be, in some way, at the root of participation so that 'primitive man' feels it and, it might be said, perceives it, as is evident from his ways of acting in so many circumstances (sympathetic magic, symbolic actions, etc. . . .).—No, because to make an appeal to some sort of anthropomorphism is too easy a way of satisfying ourselves; man feels himself, as a person, participating in his group; he projects outwards from himself this participation which thus becomes a kind of scheme for his representations and a point of application for acting on the surrounding things and objects. This explanation, which is purely hypothetical, supplies nothing new and does not help us to advance. What is needed is to hark back to the feeling of appurtenance and participation, and try to go rather deeper.

Le Minihic: August 14th, 1938.

Let us try therefore to put ourselves at a more deeply situated level, that is to say to escape entirely from the psychologist's fallacy and in no way make 'primitive man' into a 'savage philosopher'. Let us start from what he has in common with other higher animals, among which reactions to external stimuli are no longer simply reflexes and are complicated by psychological phenomena. At this level, what is more fundamental and universal is the individual organism's tendency, its effort, towards self-preservation, which in practice expresses itself through the needs felt and the modes of action proper to satisfying them: the search for food, defence against enemies, amorous passion, etc. . . . This effort towards self-preservation is at the root of the feeling which each organism has of its individuality, a feeling which, in man, tends towards a more or less distinct consciousness, more or less conscious, one might say, of this individuality. The very effort which is necessary in order to defend oneself against the causes of destruction which menace life promotes this feeling (which is also a sign and an expression of it) and tends to make it more distinct. This is an experience of which we are continually witnesses, and which we ourselves continually undergo. There is no reason to dwell further on this.

But in the case of man there is a singularity which ought to hold our attention. The individual's effort at self-preservation is not realized solely through what has been called the instinct of self-preservation and through the acts, determined by this instinct, tending to avoid the destruction of his individual organism. The effort of self-preservation includes something more and different. As an organism, he fights to save his individual existence, and he has the feeling that he does so. But at the same time, as a member of a social group, without which and outside which he would not be able to live, the effort of self-preservation is an effort toward maintaining the existence of the group in which his own is so comprised that it is not separate from it. Here, again, the effort is accompanied by a feeling, which is that of belonging to the group for the preservation of which the effort is made—not necessarily with awareness, still less intentionally and upon reflection.

In other words, for man, in even the most primitive societies, the effort of self-preservation, a primordial and direct expression of his need to live, includes the effort to maintain the existence of the *social* organism to which the individual belongs, in the full sense of the word. He feels that he continues to exist only if the social organism resists the causes of destruction; his own preservation is not separate, or distinct (except from the biological point of view) from that of this organism.

One understands, then, that for these 'primitive men', as I have shown, death may be only an event of secondary importance (Driberg), the passage to elsewhere, a change of residence. What would be tragic and dreadful would be if the new conditions of existence were to prevent the deceased from continuing to belong to his group: it would be something very different from isolation and solitude; it would be the hideous menace of annihilation, the impossibility of continuing to exist as an individual, who is nothing if he ceases to belong to the social body. At this point I concur with the profound views of Leenhardt, who explains that before contact with white men his Kanaka had neither the idea of individuality nor that of death, which are connected. Living or dead, they belong to the group, to the clan. The feeling which they have of their own existence is based on the feeling of their belonging to this group: their effort at self-preservation is therefore at the same time an effort for the preservation of this group. One also recalls those Australian aborigines, of whom Howitt, I think it is, speaks, who are not of the same clan as their father, and who, in event of conflict between two clans, fight resolutely against him.

Consequently, in the case of these 'primitive men', the effort of self-preservation is a complex in which the effort toward maintaining the existence of one's own organism necessarily occurs but also, it might be said above all, toward maintaining that of the group of which he is an element. If into this psychic complex there enters not only the feeling of this effort—in the form of emotions and of psychic expression of motivational phenomena—but elements of representations, however badly defined, these representations are related not only to the individual who wishes to live as an individual, but necessarily also to the individual as member of his group, since, for him, to live is precisely to belong intimately to this group—little matter whether it is when he is of this world or when he has passed into another.

Le Minihic: August 15th, 1938.

SOCIOLOGICAL VIEW OF THE FEELING OF PARTICIPATION

What increases the difficulty for me here is that it is not a matter of a thesis to be established or demonstrated, but only states and tendencies to be described as exactly as possible, and, on the other hand, that I do not have at my disposal an adequate vocabulary for this description. What is transmitted to me by tradition is formed by the reflections on the psychic phenomena of sensibility, perception, memory, reason, effort of will, etc. . . ., such as they occur in the consciousness where they may be observed. It is only recently that the existence and importance of the unconscious (Freud) has been recognized, and it has still only been studied in the individual. Now what we have to describe never presents itself to the mind of philosophers and psychologists who have not had the experience of individuals who, although individuals, feel themselves to be the members, the elements, of a social body which is felt and represented as the true individual; which, without doubt, is composed of its members but which, at the same time, makes them exist; which, in our language, is their *raison d'être*, their substance, since if, through misfortune, they are separated and cut off from it, the social body doubtless suffers damage, but they are lost.

In the usual descriptions of psychic life we do not find any allusions to this original idea of belonging. Naturally, sociologists have insisted on social solidarities of all kinds between individuals, on the feeling and the idea which they have of them. But they take as given *in the first place* the individual consciousnesses before showing the ties and influence which they exercise on one another. It could not have been otherwise, given the societies of which they were part, which they had before their eyes, or which were known to them. But we have to deal with elementary societies, and accordingly with different consciousnesses.

Bagatelle: August 18th, 1938.

The most striking difference is this last. At the lowest degree of feeling which the individual has of his own existence—of course without his being what we call conscious of it—this feeling embraces at one and the same time his individual existence and that of the group to which he belongs, that is to say that of other members of which the group is actually composed, that of ancestors who have passed into the other world, and that of mythical and totemic ancestors. How to express this feeling which has never been observed by philosophers and psychologists? Yet it is indeed necessary to borrow from them some terms, those that will be the least inadequate and which will entrain the fewest confusions and misunderstandings. For example, we will say that in the coenaesthesis of a 100 per cent Australian or Marindanim one would find not only the elements which our physiologists and psychologists have determined, but the feeling that the individual feels himself to belong to his group, that is to say to the living and dead members of his group, and that he relates this feeling to himself instinctively, so to speak. He relates the motor-affective phenomena, etc., of which he feels that his person is the seat and which function in him in a way which cannot fail to be recognized: the feeling of a solidarity of existence with the group presents the same character in this primitive man, and that is why one can say that it is present in his coenaesthesis.

One might also say that the feeling which the individual has of his own existence includes that of symbiosis with the other members of the group—on condition that this is not understood as an existence in common with the type of lower animals which live in colonies, but simply of existences which are felt as being in an inevitable, constant and reciprocal dependence—but one which at ordinary times is not expressly felt precisely because, like atmospheric pressure, it is constantly present. An instructive comparison: just as atmospheric pressure, of which man would never have had any suspicion if physics had not discovered it, is yet accepted without any undue difficulty, so similarly with this feeling of symbiosis which is essential to the feeling which 'primitive man' has of himself and of which he is not only unaware but which we cannot directly observe in him: it is his behaviour, his institutions, his myths, and his beliefs which give us an indubitable proof of it.

August 18th, 1938.

Notebook V
August 19th–August 27th, 1938

I might summarize the inevitably imperfect description which precedes in this formula: 'The participation of the individual in the social body is an immediate datum contained in the feeling which the individual has of his own existence.' It has the advantage of placing the accent on the *fundamental* character of this felt participation, of implying that it is not a certain particular experience, but an experience, so to speak, continuous and coextensive with the elementary feeling which the primitive individual has of himself. But it also has some drawbacks as does every other expression which is familiar to us and which we are used to seeing employed to convey a different reality. 'Immediate data', an expression celebrated since Bergson's argument, immediately give rise in the reader's mind to ideas such as those of the senses, and of the more or less clear awareness, perceptions, sensations, representations of time and space: ideas more or less directly related to the knowledge and thought of the subject. Now, when we say that participation is an immediate datum of the feeling which the individual has of his own existence, the formula involves nothing relating to knowledge or thought. We are not at the level of representations, even the most elementary ones, but at another, situated in the depths of the individual, where the phenomena which occur are undoubtedly psychic but essentially affective, although in fact the possibility of representations is not excluded: in that they are truly human.

That the feeling of participation may thus be an immediate datum of the feeling that the individual has of his own existence—outside, of course, the vaguest awareness, and, *a fortiori*, any reflection—has some important consequences. Consequently we are more in a position to understand other participations which primitive man finds very simple and natural, and which at times

83

do not fail to astonish us. For example, he makes great use of the principle *pars pro toto* (Volume VI): the head will take the place of the whole body, the lower jaw will take the place of the skull, the eye will take the place of the entire face, etc.; primitive men's designs, paintings, and plastic works leave no doubt on this point. What are their reasons for accepting that the part represents the whole? (That is to say that the presence of the part assures the real presence of the whole, or that the possession of a dead man's skull is equivalent to having the deceased in one's power.) They do not base it on anything. Their certainty is no less complete. They have no need for reason or explanation: they feel the participation between the part and the whole as they feel the participation between themselves and the social body of which they form part, and the feeling leaves no room for doubt nor for a critical attitude.

If this is so, *pars pro toto* is not a principle, nor an axiom: it is we who formulate it and who give it an abstract and conceptual expression which seems to provide a legitimation which indeed seems to be lacking from another source. For it is claimed only from our point of view. From the point of view of primitive man, it is enough that a participation be felt between the whole and what belongs to it in order for a part of this whole to represent it, or, better said, in order that the whole may be present in the part: the ancestor's skull is the ancestor himself, the lower jaw is the skull itself—exactly as the individual, full of the feeling of his participation with the other members of the social body, does not feel himself to exist without it.

Bois de Boulogne: August 19th, 1938.

'PARS PRO TOTO' INVOLVES PARTICIPATION

The formula *pars pro toto*, so clear and simple in appearance, threatens to lead us into error if we do not take the precaution of asking ourselves, as it is always prudent to do, whether it indeed has for 'primitive men' (who however do not use the formula, at least in these terms) exactly the same sense as it does for us. We find it clear and intelligible because it has a quantitative character, and most often it is supported by a spatial intuition. The part is not as large as the whole: an axiom, that is to say proposition which is so evident that it does not need to be proved; likewise the whole is composed of parts, etc. . . . Then one understands that a part may appear 'to represent the whole', that is to say to act as a sign or symbol (in the sense in which we take this word): by a sort of convention. The presence of a part, which is naturally associated with the idea of the whole, suggests this idea and in this way the logical operations become much easier. One part of the whole is actually given, that is enough, the rest are understood. The relations of the parts to the whole make possible this convenient arrangement on condition, of course, that it is a matter of a whole of which one knows, of which one sees how it is composed of its parts. In brief the formula implies that one is at a level of objects and things of which one has a sufficiently clear knowledge. Which is what signifies the fact that the part serves as 'sign' or 'symbol' of the whole.

Now, for primitive men whom we suppose make use of this formula, the sense is completely different. It is not quantitative; they are very far from thinking that the whole is composed of the sum of its parts, that each of them is smaller than it, etc. . . . In brief, the complex which is produced in them is not of a cognitive but an affective character. Parts of the whole are (taking care not to situate either it or them in space, and not to involve juxtaposition, assemblages, separation, etc.) the objects or the things which are felt as intimately participating with the whole. This condition is necessary and sufficient. If participation is in fact felt, at the same stroke it is also what I have called consubstantiality, and in a large number of cases duality-unity, that is to say the qualitative, not the quantitative, identification of the two beings or objects (words fail me precisely because one is outside the domain of knowledge), between which participation takes place.

Thus one sees that the use of the word 'part' here almost certainly entails a mistake. For us, the part can be the sign, the symbol, the representative of the whole to which it belongs; by definition, it *is not* the whole, it could not be the whole without a contradiction. For the primitive mentality, in an infinity of circumstances the part *is* the whole: we have as much proof of this as one would want in its beliefs and in its acts. That is what I had noted as early as *How Natives Think* and which incited me to say, a little prematurely, that these minds, in certain circumstances, are less sensible than ours to contradiction. A web of mis-understandings, an ever gushing source of superfluous discussions. Today—and this is doubtless progress—I no longer look for the difference between the primitive mentality and ours from the point of view of logic. But I have learned that participations do not need to be known or thought in order to be felt as real, and that in the formula 'part', 'whole', 'to be', 'to represent', etc., do not have the sense which we normally give to these words.

August 20th, 1938.

PARTICIPATIONS INDEPENDENT OF TIME AND SPACE

These essential characteristics of participation can be expressed in a slightly different way again. In spite of the place which participation occupies in the mental life and even in the modes of activity of 'primitive men', it is never either perceived or con-ceived by them. Not perceived, that goes without saying: there is nothing in participation which is perceptible through the senses. Doubtless it is felt, but not in the form of sensation as smells and colours are: it is a feeling *sui generis, iudex sui*, like that which occurs when the affective category of the supernatural comes into action.—Not conceived, this is no less evident as it were *a priori*, since far from it being possible to have a concept of participation, the understanding, on the contrary, makes it diffi-cult to accept that participation can be real, and declines to 'justify' claims which no analysis can manage to make intelligible (Bororo—the 3 graves of Junod, the bi-presence of the living, and that of the dead, etc.).

Consequence: having no need of being either perceived or conceived, participations remain independent of the general and universal conditions of objectivity, of the conditions under which reality is necessarily given, that is to say without which conditions what is felt or perceived cannot be real. For example, the enemy in possession of the chief's portrait, or of the dead chief's skull, has at his mercy the tribe's fortune. How to represent the relation between the tribe's well-being and the portrait or the skull? The portrait may have been transported some thousands of kilometres away. How to represent the relation between the skull and the chief who has gone to live with other clan members in the other world, how to represent the repercussion on the chief, and secondarily on the tribe of what is done to the skull? The determinations in space and time which are indispensable in order for facts to have a place in the series of real phenomena are here entirely lacking, or, what amounts to the same thing, escape us completely, are imperceptible to us: whence it follows that partici-pations are outside the phenomenal, causal nexus, the latter being conceivable here without the well-ordered series of phenomena in time, where the before and the after are determined unam-biguously, and are irreversible. Another example: the Naga and his leopard (and other similar and numerous facts). The leopard is wounded, killed: the Naga bears the wound on his body and dies. An action has been exercised on him, when he was not there. The death of an animal distinct from him results in his death. We will no longer say, as we did in *How Natives Think,* that here is something absurd, impossible, which shows the primitive mentality to be indifferent to contradiction and to tolerate it. The bi-presence, the duality-unity do not involve a contradiction strictly understood. But we are obliged to recognize that some facts of this sort, which the primitive mentality con-siders to be perfectly real and undoubtable, appear to us to be incompatible with the indispensable conditions of all reality. Therefore let us not be surprised that they are neither perceived nor conceived: they *cannot* be.

But then, participations are not truly facts. They are in vain to be felt as real, with complete certainty, they are not experiences of the primitive mentality. They are not 'data', they are beliefs which tradition and the pressure of the social milieu impose and which are subjectively equivalent to some experiences.

August 21st, 1938.

PARTICIPATION, MYSTICAL EXPERIENCE AND BELIEF

We do not have to search for how participations, although not perceived and not conceived, are meanwhile perfectly real for the primitive mentality: Volume VI has shown how, in primitive men's experiences, intermixed with the experience which is common to us and them occurs constantly another experience which we call mystical,—an experience as real as the other in

H

their eyes but which, in ours, lacks that which makes it objective (save in the case of religious experience properly so called).

It will be worth the effort to take advantage of this example, and to examine the reasons why, in the eyes of 'primitive men', the mystical experience has no less, if not more, value than the other, and to ask if these are not the same reasons, or reasons of the same type, that make participation felt as real by the primitive mentality. What ensures a mystical experience a value which no one has the slightest idea of doubting is that it gives the unmistakable feeling of a direct and immediate contact with a being, a force, etc., of the invisible world, of which the reality and presence are accepted as it were in advance: (the shark of the Kanaka, the relations with the dead, in dreams or otherwise, etc.). When 'primitive man' feels a participation as real is the case the same, can the fact be assimilated to a mystical experience; and if there is a difference, of what does this difference consist?

The Australian is persuaded that there is between the footprint and the individual whose foot has imprinted the steps a close participation, so that the action performed on the footprint operates simultaneously on the individual himself, however distant he may be. Is this a mystical experience? No, we are inclined to reply at first. The only experience which occurs is the participation of the footprints, which the Australian recognizes immediately as those of such and such an individual (human or animal). Nobody will say that the Australian has the truly mystical experience because the blow from the spear which pierces the footprints pierces at the same time the foot which made them. One will say that he believes in this action because he believes in a close participation between the individual and his footprints.

And yet here is indeed a mystical experience of participation. What prevents us from seeing it is that, without thinking about it, we substitute our own mental attitude for that of the Australian, failing to make the necessary effort sincerely to adopt his, except in words, and to hold ourselves to it. For us, the footprints in the sand are a depression of which the contour recalls immediately the shape of the foot which has imprinted them. The relationship between this depression in the sand and the individual whose foot has made it is grasped by the mind which immediately connects them. We do not see anything else there, and we know that there is nothing more to see there. The footprints may exist for a shorter or longer length of time, be blurred or effaced by the wind, etc., the individual who left them will be neither the better nor the worse for it.

This attitude which is ours, and which seems to us the only reasonable one (we do not imagine another!) is not at all that of the Australian. When the footprints catch his eye, they do not simply suggest to him the idea of the individual whose foot has imprinted them in the sand. The presence of the footprints is *ipso facto* for him the presence of that individual: he *feels* this presence of the individual, although he may be far away and invisible, *as existing* by virtue of the participation between him and his footstep. In brief, if participation is not a word but a reality, in the full sense of the term (which it is in effect for the Australian), we are indeed obliged to recognize here a mystical experience.

Doubtless, might it be said, for the Australian the participation between the footprints and the individual is real. But it does not follow that he has the actual, even mystical, experience of this reality. Is it not enough to say that he believes it? Since his earliest childhood, he has been imbued with the belief in participations of all sorts: this belief is shared by all those who surround him, it is the reason for a large number of their customs and methods, from which the return seems satisfying. That confirms the reality of the participations, and proves, not that he has the actual experience, but that his belief is well founded. Moreover, except for certain universally accepted participations (for example, the participation between an individual and his immediate appurtenances, his name, his reflection, his shadow, etc.), there are those which are taken as real in certain societies and which are ignored in others: thus the participation of which we were speaking just now, between the footprints and the individual who left them, is known only in Australia, New Guinea and some other primitive societies. If the feeling of it was given through an actual mystical experience, ought it not to be everywhere? . . . Doubtless, we reply, on this last point, following the conception which we have of direct experience, which is the same for all men. But what if it is a matter of mystical experience? We have seen in Volume VI that for this it is not necessarily so. In a single small group, no one is surprised that certain people, or only one has some privileged mystical experiences which the others do not have. Therefore it is no more surprising that certain mystical

experiences occur in this primitive society, and do not occur in
some other. Therefore little matter that such or such a particular
participation is accepted here and not there, above all when, here
as there, a large number of participations cause no doubt.

The other objection is more serious. Is a strong unanimous
belief enough to explain why some participations are considered
as real? And, if it is so, what need is there to base the feeling of
this reality in a mystical experience?

... A beginning of an answer to this important point has
already been indicated in Volume VI (facts from Hallowell,
and reflections on the difficulty of distinguishing belief from
experience). To us, on the contrary, it seems that there would be
much lack of good will to confuse them: we know very well when
we experience something, or when we only believe it. But what
we have in mind is the positive experience and the characteristics
which form the objectivity of it, characteristics very different
from those of a thing which is simply an object of belief. If it is
a matter of a mystical experience which may be truly an experience but which has no need to present the characteristics
proper to the positive experience, the position changes and the
distinction between belief and mystical experience tends, in a
large number of cases, to become attenuated and even to disappear. Is the reality of what is seen and felt while dreaming
an act of belief or a mystical experience? In our societies, the
answer to this question will vary according to the circumstances
of the dream and the people questioned; in the societies called
primitive, generally the question will not even be posed.

August 22nd, 1938.

AFFECTIVITY, THE GENERAL ELEMENT IN PARTICIPATION

The effort for us to explain what participation is is condemned
perhaps to remain unavailing. In every case, if there is some
chance of attaining a positive result it is on condition that the
search for anything which resembles a conceptual form, a scheme
of organized or organizing thought, a principle of generality
relevant to the understanding is avoided. Just as in the study of
the affective category of the supernatural I have always taken
care to insist on the point that 'category' did not imply the

sense of Aristotle's and Kant's categories, and that, if there was an element of generality, it consisted solely in the uniformity of the characteristic emotion which is produced when this category comes into action,—likewise, if our starting point is a law or principle of participation, we must guard ourselves against implying what these words, principle and law, usually entail, and never lose from sight that participations, always private, are felt, and not thought. The general element, if there is one other than that which our thought introduces into it, can therefore only be found in the uniform way, always the same, in which a participation is felt.

Pré-Catelan: August 24th, 1938.

If the primitive mentality feels participations, they are not therefore in any way products of the mind's mental activity, and the element of generality which they present can therefore only be an aspect of their uniformity. But then, if this is so, two different questions are set us.

1. Whence comes this uniformity? 2. How comes it that certain participations are felt (between the individual and his group and the country which it inhabits and what that country produces, between the individual and his appurtenances, between the Naga and his leopard, etc.?) and not others?

For a reply to this second question we are put on the right road by what has been said in Volume VI concerning the relations of belief and experience (account taken of the sense which the words ought to have when it is a matter of the primitive mentality). We have seen that if the mystical experience is revelation, from the very fact of the emotion which is inseparable from it, this revelation yet reveals nothing but this same emotion, and that a presence or an action of an invisible force is thus revealed: if it is an intuition, it is implicit. If therefore mystical experiences are rich in positive content, at least as rich as the positive experience, this content comes from elsewhere. We know from where; it comes from the beliefs relating to the invisible world, which are imprinted in all the minds of the group by the language, tradition, myths of which the sacred character is the foundation of the objective value and authority (cf. dreams). As has been explained, it is impossible not to take, on each particular occasion, the traditional belief of this type for a real experience (Hallowell).

In the same way, if we envisage *in concreto* the particular participations felt by the primitive mentality in such and such society we will be able to explain them, as we have done for mystical experiences in showing that the traditions, myths and beliefs of which they are. I will not say an expression (that would entice us onto the level of knowledge) but a translation, an echo, a *Nachklang* in the domain of the felt. So that the uniformity of participations in so far as they are felt is perfectly compatible with the diversity of participations (appurtenances, bi-presence, duality-unity, etc.). Here there appears an essential difference between participation and causality. The latter a category of understanding, the former a feeling felt, and of an objectivity otherwise founded.

Pré-Catelan: August 24th, 1938.

If it is thus, one sees immediately why it is preferable, on the subject of participation, to abstain from speaking of 'law' or 'principle'. With these terms, whatever one does, whatever precaution one may resolve to take, a 'set of laws' is implied, an order imposed on the facts, an intelligibility given with their very perception. It is to enter a dead end, or at very least on the wrong road.

Therefore there remains simply the question: How is it that so many participations are felt as real by the primitive mentality which are not by ours? Since the answer is not to be found in a particular form of mental activity (law, principle, general scheme, etc.), it is accordingly necessary for us to turn to the content of the feelings of participation (between the individual and the other members of his group, living or dead, between them and their mythic ancestors, between the individual and his appurtenances, between the Naga and his leopard, etc.). Now this content is clearly of social origin (traditions, legends, myths). The participations felt by each individual are therefore closely linked to the representation or to the feeling of the mythical world taken as real.

August 25th, 1938.

8 1938

In other words, the numerous participations felt by the primitive mentality and of which its symbolical and magical modes of action make such constant use, which proves so well the confidence which it has in the reality of these participations, are the natural, spontaneous and decisive illustration of what I explained in Volume VI; the mystical experience and the positive experience, although the primitive mentality can distinguish them in so far as they are not felt qualitatively in the same way, yet form only one and the same experience, for they are closely intertwined and penetrate one another. In general, the 'primitive man' takes as example for his behaviour the objective and verifiable experience: it is indeed necessary in order that he may live and escape from the multiple causes of destruction that he adapt himself in the best way he can to the conditions of existence which the surrounding milieu imposes on him. In this he acts like other living beings and more especially like the other higher animals, with superiority in the choice of means and in the modes of adaptation which intelligence, language, life in society and tradition assure him. But at the same time, these real objects to which he adapts his behaviour exist for him from yet another point of view than that of practical needs. He has a disinterested feeling—at least for the most part—in their existence and in the relations between them and him. It is that which forms the content of myths and the substance of mystical experience. Thus he lives in two worlds which form only one, if one prefers it, in a world which is at one and the same time unique and double: unique in so far as it is visible and tangible—double in as much as it is at the same time invisible and multiple participations are felt there, of which it will not be said that they 'explain' the reasons for the existence of things but that they recount their origin and transformations, and make known the details and relationships.

To demonstrate this by the facts. Take the example analysed earlier of the participation of the 'primitive man' with his group, with the earth, with the mythical ancestors. The two aspects in question jump into view. The lessons of ordinary daily experience teach him how he ought to behave in his relations with the other individuals of the group, and he normally conforms well enough in this in order that life in society may be possible and even satisfying without police and organized judicial machinery. As is proper, he cares for his self-respect, observes the traditional rules, practises fair play and *do ut des*. Even behaves in a way which we judge rational, or at least sensible, in what concerns hunting, fishing, agriculture, war, relations with other tribes, etc. . . .

But on looking at this very closely, a whole rich and complex life of mystical character and extreme importance appears. This same Australian has not only the behaviour of which we have just spoken in his relations with the other members of the tribe and the surrounding environment (recall the 'secret life' described in Volumes V and VI), but as many felt participations which are the essential conditions for the existence of the group and of each of those who compose it. Now, the point, on which I must here insist, is that primitive man *feels* and *lives* these essential participations, but he does not define them, does not separate them from his person, and does not have the idea of objectifying them. It is the observer who points them out, characterizes them, defines them and delimits their function. The Australian himself is barely more aware of them than the fact that he breathes and digests. To the extent that he has the feeling of his own individual existence, he has at the same time the feeling of his participation with his group and with the ancestors (initiation, etc.).

Here we can hark back to the relations of belief and experience and show how, in our language, they mutually reinforce themselves or, leaving aside this language, how from the point of view of the most archaic primitive mentality they are difficult to distinguish. Doubtless possible for us, the Australian would not feel these participations, whether with his group, his clan, his totem (ceremonies, initiation, local relationship, etc.) if the myths had not taught him what they are, in themselves, and in their relations with him, the mythical ancestors, the clan kinsmen, etc.: If he were ignorant of them, would these participations exist for him? But mutually, the intensity of feeling which he has of these participations is the most powerful support of the myths' reality. For the Australian, in ceremonies and often even in ordinary life, has the actual experience of the participations. He does not think them, he lives them: it is not enough, nor correct to say that he believes in the myths of which participations are for him the realization in his experience of what has been realized in the mythic period.

This function of participations illuminates in a striking way the indispensable role of precedents, which Volume VI made clear. The primitive mentality has no need of causes, in the sense in which we take the word, in order to explain its mystical experiences. It has need only of precedents, thanks to which the participation actually felt is based on a similar participation of the mythical period, the sacred character of which ensures that it is legitimate. Therefore there is no need to go further, and there is no idea of resorting to an endless regression, like that which causal series in time involve. In this way, on the one hand, myths are the *raison d'être* of the individual's participations, and 'legitimates' them to the extent that they are in need of legitimation— and, on the other hand, the actual experience of participations, experienced and felt, confirms the myths, if they are in need of it.

Bagatelle: August 25th, 1938.

PARTICIPATION BETWEEN ONE AND MANY: INVERSE THE PROBLEM

The important facts reported in the legends of the Tartars of central Asia by N. Chadwick, and his reflections on these facts and on shamanism. He insists on the point that some spiritual beings (supposed inhabitants of the sky, or the subterranean world) are represented at one and the same time as individuals and collectivities. The swan woman is at one time a person, at another time the seven or nine *bird souls* who are her attendants. (Cf. Wirz, the followers who in the myths accompany the *dema*.) This 'alternation' between the individuality of the swan woman and her plurality does not seem to offer any difficulty to the Tartars, who adapt themselves to it very well. Nevertheless it is at least strange to western minds.

Perhaps it could be explained by some archaic beliefs and institutions, in which a plurality of persons acts as a single individual: in Tibet, a number of brothers are only a single husband for one woman (it would be possible to find without difficulty better alternations). But the author adds: it is evident that it is not a question here solely of the social organization, but of something far more subtle, which has dropped out of the

European mind. Which tends to prove: 1. that the problem of
participation as I pose it, that is to say as essential for the understanding of the primitive mentality, is not something arbitrary,
but necessarily follows from facts well attested in the most diverse
societies; 2. that the strictly sociological solution, if not wrong, is
inadequate in any case.

Perhaps we would be on the way to a solution of the sort
which Chadwick asks for, if we were to try to make use of her
way of revealing the facts. She has been led to her thoughts by
consideration of beliefs relating to the external soul. The latter,
generally, shows itself in the form of a bird, but also as many
birds. The seven or nine (birds) of the swan woman are her
external soul, that is to say, from a certain point of view they *are*
she. In the legend, in order to kill her it is necessary to wring the
necks of these seven or nine swans. When they are all dead,
she also is dead.

Thus the problem: individuality-plurality is simply another
aspect of the problem of participation between an individual and
his external soul (an unfortunate expression, only because of the
confusions heaped on the word soul); one could besides say:
between a thing and its double, its symbol, its substitute (cf.
Volumes V and VI) or between a person and his bush-soul
(Kingsley) or between the Naga and his leopard, or between the
European peasant and the were-wolf of which he sometimes takes
the form, etc. . . . What western thought does not manage to
understand is that a single being can be found, at one and the
same time, in different places in different forms (Naga-leopard).
It understands very well that the same insect may be at a given
moment of its life a caterpillar, and at another a butterfly, and
likewise the changes of shell-fish, etc. . . . But a duality or plurality,
actual and simultaneous, seems to it incompatible with individuality. If the Naga is a man, how might he be at the same time
a leopard?

To seek if there might not be here something fundamental,
essential to the human mind which has the privilege, as I have
shown (Volume VI, p. 96), of representing, or at least of feeling,
the *power to be otherwise*, for which things and beings have a
double reality, one visible and one invisible. From this property
of the mind religion and science have arisen in the course of
millennia: but after how many mistakes, tentative gropings, and

absurdities! Not to believe that a sort of internal finalism directs the mental development in human societies, any more than an intelligible finality directs the evolution of organisms, although it may be equally impossible to make an abstraction of every idea of mental or biological organization (recall Hume's and Comte's principle of the conditions of existence).

Let us use these general views for the problem, itself very general, which occupies us. The constant and intense preoccupation with invisible powers (which manifest themselves so often in visible forms: for example, the animals which are not truly animals, the Kanaima jaguar, the shark of the Kanaka, the crocodile at Conakry, and *tutti quanti*) has accustomed man to pay much more attention to this duality which can be so dangerous for him than to the individuality of each being, doubtless evident and of which he takes necessary account in his behaviour. What is given for him in experience is not, as it is for us, either male or female individuals, it is the couple or the plurality: such a man or such a woman and his or her double (which one calls the external soul, symbol, bush-soul, etc., none of these expressions being adequate moreover). That is the direct and indubitable consequence of the fact that his experience, different from ours, comprehends at one and the same time what we call the positive experience and the mystical experience, and that for obvious reasons, he is more preoccupied with the latter than the former.

If, as is advisable, the wording is inversed, the problem then ceases to appear insoluble. In place of asking: How in the primitive mentality a woman can be a swan? How a Naga can be a leopard? etc., one recognizes that originally man felt and afterwards represented to himself beings who, at the same moment, were simultaneously humans, and animals or plants, or rocks, etc. . . . One will ask oneself: How the invisible reality, how the mystical experience, without disappearing, have taken forms very different from those of primitive men? How the mind has freed itself from seeing and feeling everywhere participations between things given in positive experience and those same things given in the mystical experience either actual or always possible? Then the history of societies, in particular that of myths, traditions, archaic institutions, to the degree that it will illuminate the past (at least as far as the documents which will be at one's disposal will allow), will be able to put the problems in precise terms and attempt more or less approximate solutions; and at the same time it will show why the primitive mentality finds completely natural what seems so strange to us.

For the primitive mentality, without having to think about it, participations are everywhere from the sole fact that its experience is what it is and that all things have an invisible as well as visible existence—and it is thus irrelevant to ask how they are established and started for the primitive mentality. On the contrary it is necessary to seek how they are little by little effaced and destroyed. Thus they are not to be considered at the level of logic or by the theory of cognition (*Erkenntnistheorie*). It is a question of evolution, of history, of social psychology.

It would be too risky to compare with these considerations the fact which has always seemed to me of such significance (although, until now, I should have been at a loss to say why)—the fact that in primitive societies one is not a number. Numeration begins with 'two'. We do not conceive of numbers otherwise than as composites based on the units, and this is true for numbers conceived abstractly. But, in fact, they began by being concrete and inseparable, or at least unseparated from the things that were enumerated. If what is given in the beginning are dualities and pluralities, one could not at first be a number.

Bagatelle: August 27th, 1938.

Notebook VI

August–September 1938

PRESENT POSITION COMPARED WITH THE OLD ONE:
ABANDONMENT OF 'PRELOGICAL'

The step which I have just taken, and hope is decisive, consists, in a word, in abandoning a badly posed problem, which resulted in some inextricable difficulties, and in confining myself to a question the terms of which are suggested by the facts alone. Until now, I had not entirely renounced the assumptions (*Voraussetzungen*) fixed in my mind at the time of writing *How Natives Think* and which dominated its composition. There is no doubt that for some time I have not spoken of a logic other than our own, nor used the term 'prelogical', and have given up speaking of the law of participation. But the very essence of this idea exists without this form; participation still seemed to me to be something essential to the primitive mentality, and probably to the human mind, making a complement and perhaps a counterweight to the regulating principles of logical thought. But if this is so, where does participation's field of action begin and end? How can one understand that it might be something essential to the structure of the human mind, which necessarily intervenes in the representation which the mind forms of objects and things, and whose function has had to wait until the twentieth century to be recorded? That neither psychologists, nor logicians, nor even metaphysicians such as Plato and Malebranche, who have spoken, and excellently, on certain participations, have attributed to it the function in the mind which was recognized in *How Natives Think*? And, since it seems that participation involves something deeply rebellious to intelligibility, how is one to understand that the human mind could be at one and the same time the mainspring of the rational and irrational?

From this it follows that, even allowing for the numerous and characteristic cases of participation of which my six volumes are

99

full, there still exist doubts about the explanation—even as
modestly reduced in Volumes V and VI—I have given of them
in invoking the presence of mental habits different from ours
among 'primitive peoples'. But, even with these conclusions, I
still want to account for participation, if not from the logical
point of view, at least from the viewpoint of the knowledge of
objects, and of their understanding—while recognizing that this
understanding, when it concerns participations, entails an important part of affective, not cognitive, elements. And the question
reappears: 'How does it happen that these "mental habits"
make themselves felt in certain circumstances and not in others?
What is that had so determined, in the human mind, two orienta-
tions different to the point that when it represents or feels
participations, the impossibility of making them intelligible
causes in it a discomfort which it can neither hide nor surmount?'
It is to suppose in the mental structure a deep-seated discord
worse than all paradoxes. There is no solution here to the problem
posed; it is rather a confession that one does not have the solution,
and an indication that perhaps one has not got it because the
problem is badly posed.

If I glance over all I have written on the subject of participation between 1910 and 1938, the development of my ideas seems
clear to me. I started by positing a primitive mentality different
from ours, if not in its structure at least in its function, and I
found myself in difficulties in explaining the relationships with
the other mentality, not only among us but also among 'primitive
peoples'. In short, I had only juxtaposed them, without being
able to account for either their coexistence or their relations. A
position which I have never been able to defend well, and in the
long run an untenable one. By limiting myself to discussing
mental customs, I took refuge in withdrawal. But the thesis thus
extenuated and weakened is no more defensible. One will then
ask whence these customs arise, and how, in themselves, they
constitute a 'mentality' which, in an inexplicable fashion, coexists with the logical exercise of our mental activity.

Let us then give up this retreat in its turn and without reservation, that is to say, let us entirely give up explaining participation
by something peculiar to the human mind, either constitutional
(in its structure or function) or acquired (mental customs). In
other words, let us expressly rectify what I believed correct in

1910: there is not a primitive mentality distinguishable from the other by *two* characteristics which are peculiar to it (mystical and prelogical). There is a mystical mentality which is more marked and more easily observable among 'primitive peoples' than in our own societies, but it is present in every human mind. From the moment that it is no longer set up as something which is opposed to a different mentality, all the above problems disappear.

Bagatelle: August 29th, 1938.

Once the obstructing hypotheses have been brushed aside, we no longer have to ask ourselves: 'What is this participation which the primitive mentality (of the human mind) feels and apprehends between objects and beings? Why does it feel it on such an occasion and not on another?' We put ourselves simply on the level of facts. Let us study in what circumstances and under what conditions, primitive peoples (and we ourselves) feel and represent participations. Perhaps the very simple reason why, in other circumstances and under other conditions, participation has no role to play will emerge directly from this study.

This study is not entirely new to us; there is in what we have said about the primitive mentality, from Volume I to Volume VI, a quantity of data which we can take into account. For example, there remains what we used to call primitive mentality, characterized by its mystical orientation, and that this last, in fact, seems to be accompanied usually by participations, felt or represented. There remains the affective category of the supernatural, which since Volume VI I have been unable to do without, and particularly Volumes V and VI (mythical thought, mystical experience) involve participations above all. It is from here that it is now necessary to make a start.

Bagatelle: August 29th, 1938.

The preceding considerations have the advantage of making clear my present position, of specifying for myself how my ideas on the primitive mentality—in particular on its difference from ours from the logical point of view—have been modified little by little, and how I have renounced certain equivocal or inexact formulae; in brief, of showing me as exactly as possible where I am at this moment. But they go no further. They do not suggest anything fruitful which may lead, I do not say to understanding participation—since it seems to be by its nature not understandable, but to giving account of the fact that it holds so great a place in the primitive mentality, of its different forms, etc. . . .

Yet there is a general remark which perhaps provides a starting point. Participation seems—with certain exceptions—linked to mystical experience. Or, if one prefers it, mystical experience seems to involve participation. It is to the degree of having mystical experiences that primitive man would feel as real participations between himself and the things which surround him, or between those things. If this is so, the conditions on which mystical experience depends would be like those on which participations depend.

Thus one would see why one would take the wrong road in wishing, very strongly, to discover a principle of the human mind which is at the base of the participations which it believes to establish, forming, in some way, a pair with the principle of identity and the principle of causality. It is necessary to abandon the search for a principle of this type (that is to say to stop looking at it from a logical point of view or that of the theory of cognition) and to remain at the level of the mystical experience: consequently to search for the conditions under which this experience takes place. From the same action, some light would be thrown on participation.

Now this is an analysis with which I proceeded as best I could in Volume VI, and it is evident there that there is barely a mystical experience which does not involve the feeling and the experience of a participation. In effect, the essence of every mystical experience is the feeling (accompanied by a characteristic emotion *sui generis*) of the presence, and often of the action of an invisible power, the feeling of a contact, most often unforeseen, with a reality other than the reality given in the surrounding milieu. It is the revelation of this other reality, not of its existence, in which the 'primitive man' believes from his earliest years and of which he has already had the [actual] experience many times, but of its actual presence. And as it is not a question here of knowledge but of an experience of an essentially affective character, the 'primitive man' feels that he is dealing, not with a uniform and homogeneous reality, but with a complex reality where those things which he is accustomed to perceive in the surrounding milieu to which he is adapted, and those things which he is accustomed to see manifest themselves to him through the revelation which constitutes the mystical experience are intertwined and interlaced. The fact, which I tried to make clear in Volume VI, that both sets of things intermix continually, that although felt as qualitatively distinct yet are at the same time only a single and unique experience, is expressed in 'primitive man' through the feeling of participation. The interpenetration of what we call two experiences, the positive and the mystical, of two realities, the visible and the invisible, if we consider the interpenetration in the objects which compose these realities, in the content of these experiences, appears as a participation between certain objects belonging to one and certain other objects belonging to the other.

And let us not say that we thus obtain the prototype, archetype, the general scheme of participation which plays so great a role in the thought and modes of action of 'primitive men'. This would be to put us on the level of representation, of what is thought, that is to say more or less clearly classified, ordered, conceived. We are not there yet. In what has just been explained, it is still a question of participation only in so far as it is 'felt', considered, provisionally at least, in its essentially affective nature. If I am not wrong, a point of capital importance would be achieved. As far as we are permitted to go back into observable primitive societies, and, by extrapolation, into those which preceded them, man has had the revelation that the reality is such as he sees it and at the same time there exists another reality, or, better said, that the reality given to him is at one and the same time what it is and other than what it is. The feeling of this duality-unity (which barely happens without emotions to which 'primitive man' has in vain been accustomed, for he is always more or less shaken by them) naturally cannot be something general and abstract (that would be to slip back again to the cognitive level: here the generality can only be the uniformity (in the main) of the emotion), and can therefore in practice be only the concrete and particular feeling of such and such a participation, implied in the concrete experience itself.

Bagatelle: August 31st, 1938.

I

PARTICIPATION IS NOT A LOGICAL FUNCTION

A direct consequence, and at the same time confirmation of what
precedes. One sees immediately why the simple observation of the
facts of primitive mentality seems to suggest that participation
is something inherent if not in its structure at least in its activity,
which characterizes the primitive mentality in what is most
peculiar and essential to it, and how in consequence I have been
led to conclude too quickly from this observation of the facts in
favour of a 'prelogical' character of the primitive mentality. I
understand the facts better today, and I have recognized, first
that participation did not belong exclusively to the primitive
mentality but held also a place in our own, or, if one prefers, that
the primitive mentality is in reality an aspect, a condition (Mari-
tain) of human mentality in general; second that it is not from
the logical point of view that we must study participation, since
despite appearances, there is neither law nor principle of participation.

Yet whence arise these appearances? It is indeed necessary that
they have a reason. In effect, they do have one, and the preceding
pages have indicated it. The mystical orientation of the primitive
mentality and the indestructible nature of the mystical experience
in mental life have appeared more and more clearly as primordial.
As the mystical character of the primitive mentality more clearly
and more obviously emerged, the 'prelogical' character which
was on a par with it in *How Natives Think* became uncertain,
vulnerable, and at length more than difficult to maintain, and,
in the end, disappeared. But it did not disappear entirely. The
mistake had been to establish for it a character parallel to the
mystical character, or, at very least, distinct from it through its
logical affinities. It remains no less true: first that the primitive
mentality, precisely in so far as it is mystical (in so far as it
embraces in its experience at one and the same time the positive
and mystical experiences, that is to say the feeling of and the
contact with a reality other than that of the surrounding environment), has the continually repeated feeling of participations which
impose themselves upon it; second that these participations, when,
in the course of time, after centuries of having been felt almost
exclusively and having presented no difficulty, become more and

more consciously represented, and awake a sort of need, at first timid, to justify themselves from a logical point of view, which raises some insurmountable difficulties (through the very nature of participation and its close connection with mystical experience), as the history of religion and metaphysics superabundantly proves. Research to be done: to analyse the passage from felt participation to represented participation.

Bagatelle: August 31st, 1938.

Of the two points of view just indicated, the first is not new. I have been led to touch on it in the introduction to Volume III because of the important role which I found myself obliged to recognize in it. I did it in the following form: I introduced what I have called the affective category of the supernatural, and I have shown its characteristics and great importance in the activity of the primitive mentality. But at the same time I have had the feeling that this 'affective category' was without foundation, and that I did not explain either whence it proceeded or to what it was connected. This made one suspect here something arbitrary, and simply a rather poor name given to a collection of facts: but a name adds nothing more to our analysis or to our explanation of the facts. If I remember well, Leenhardt, always clairvoyant, said to me one day: 'The affective category of the supernatural, isn't it participation?' I did not deny it, but at that very moment I did not see clearly what appeared evident to him—without doubt because I had not reflected sufficiently on participation, and because I was still under the influence of the assumption (*Voraussetzung*) which made it a principle or a law akin to logical principles, without seeing however the relation which might exist between logical principles and participation.

Without realizing it myself, I introduced this factor under a new guise: the affective category of the supernatural. What I started to feel if not to see clearly is that participation ought to be understood otherwise than I had until then; that it was in no way allied, even by opposition, to logical principles, and that, essentially, it was something felt (on which 'affective' puts the accent) while remaining something fundamental to the activity of the primitive mentality. Now that I am free of the false position adopted in *How Natives Think*, now that I see that the

assumption underlying that position ought to be abandoned, I
am able to bring myself unreservedly round to Leenhardt's profound remark and to say with him: 'The affective category of
the supernatural is participation.' In fact, the affective category
of the supernatural has served as a bridge, as a transition between
my way of 'understanding' participation in 1910 and my way
today. This duty done, it has nothing more to do and accordingly
has only to disappear. It seems to me that it would not be
unprofitable to make this confession, of recognizing that it is a
useless mechanism, and that with more clear-sightedness I would
have never thought to introduce it. It has no other interest than
that, very personal one, of marking a stage in my thought on the
subject of participation and mystical experience.

Second, when I insist on the point that, in order to explain
participation, it is necessary to take great care to stay on the
affective level and not to fall into the temptation of letting
oneself slide into the cognitive level in order to render it 'intelligible', it is necessary not to lose from view any longer that the
representations are one thing, and the connections—the pre-
connections—between the representations are another thing. Now
when one speaks of participation, it is a matter of consubstantiality, of communion, of an identity even (duality-unity) between
things and objects. What is not represented, generally, is the
close relation, so characteristic, between these things and these
objects. The relation is felt; but the objects themselves are
represented.

Thus in a society where totemism is fully operative, the members of the Lion clan feel themselves not only kinsmen of the
actually existing lions, but participating with them and like
them in a single natural community with the common totemic
ancestor, and they do not, properly speaking, represent this
participation. But they represent perfectly well the lions, and
the human group allied to them. What proves that participation
is indeed on the affective level is that the clarity of the representation of individuals or objects (lions and human beings in the
example cited) is of no help when 'primitive men' begin trying to
represent participations which until then they were happy to feel.
Generally, there is nothing to be derived from either the concept
or the image of the things which makes their participation
intelligible (Bororo-parrot, etc. . . .).

Let us examine whether there might not be here one of the profound reasons for the formation of myths. In fact, it follows from Volume V that there exists the closest relations between mythical thought and felt participations (Australia, New Guinea, etc. . . .).

September 2nd, 1938.

PARTICIPATION AND POSSESSIVE PRONOUNS

In order, I will not say to explain but rather to illustrate what participation is in the case of appurtenances, the facts of language are valuable. In a large number of 'primitive languages (Oceania, the Americas, etc. . . .) names designating parts of the body (foot, hand, head, eye, ear, etc. . . .) are not met except accompanied by a possessive pronoun. One never says foot or hand, but always my foot, your hand, the head of someone, etc. . . .

The fact is already important, but one can press it harder, and grasp how participation is felt. For example, in a number of Melanesian languages *natugu* or *natuku* means my finger. *Gu* or *ku* is regarded as a possessive pronoun. In fact it is a personal pronoun. The literal translation of *natugu* is: finger of me. What the compound word expresses is not only that the finger in question is mine, and not someone else's, it also expresses and perhaps above all that this finger is me through participation (in the sense where to be is equivalent to to participate). Which explains the particular sensitivity of primitive men on the subject of their appurtenances and the use which they make in this case of *Pars pro toto*.

September 4th, 1938.

So far as it is a matter of organs and parts of the body, this participation so expressed contains nothing to check us, because we also feel it, as 'primitive men' do, although we employ possessive pronouns, distinct from personal pronouns:—my foot, your hand—and although the names are not obligatorily accompanied by pronouns. But if it is a question of appurtenances which are not an integral part of the individual, participation (which, in general, does not entail the use of the pronoun) no longer seems to us something so natural, so matter-of-course. Thus the reflection of an individual, his urine, his footprints. Is this footprint the kangaroo itself? Yes and no. No, seeing that the animal is far away and yet the hunter is in control of the footprint. Yes, seeing that the wound inflicted on the footprint affects the animal. The needle which pierces the portrait's heart also pierces the heart of the model who is at a distance. The portrait *is* the model in the sense that to be equals to to participate, which we do not have the means to analyse undoubtedly because participation is independent of the logical and physical conditions of possibility which are imposed on our thought.

September, 1938.

DIFFERENT SORTS OF PARTICIPATIONS

The study of participation, that is to say of its function in the primitive mentality, ought not to be limited to showing its relations with the mystical experience, the affective category of the supernatural, mythical thought and traditional beliefs at the same time as one defines, so far as possible, its non-cognitive but essentially affective nature. When one has set forth and put in order what may be called participation '*überhaupt*', it is right to consider it in greater detail, not just in so far as it is opposed to other forms or products of 'primitive men's' mental activity, but putting aside all comparison, to apply oneself to the facts of participation in order to try to analyse them more closely and, as far as possible, to classify them.

1. It seems that two principal sorts of participation may be distinguished. A. Participation equals community of essence, identity felt between what participates and what is 'participated in'. Examples: participation between [the] individual and his appurtenances (hair, nails, excretions, clothing, footprints, shadow, etc. . . .)—between symbol and what it represents (stone symbols of ancestors, petrified ancestors) between corpse and ghost, at least, for a certain period; between the member of a totemic clan and the other members of the clan, living or dead, the mythical ancestor common to this clan and to his totem, etc. . . .

B. Participation equals imitation, studied in Volumes V and

VI. The indispensable function of precedents and models; basis of realities actually given, in the mythic beings; legitimation, at once mystical and historical, or rather meta-historical, which satisfies the need for explanation (not very acute however) through its definite character (there is nothing further to seek when the myth has spoken).

Show the use which 'primitive men' make, in action, of these two sorts of participation: for example, participation-community of essence: *pars pro toto*, symbolic action, etc. . . .—For participation-imitation from the negative point of view: misoneism (to deny what is not legitimated by a precedent, tradition, myth); from the positive point of view, confidence in the prefiguration (Volume VI). Study the relation of the interaction of these two sorts of participation; how, while appearing different in their principle, since they are based on two sorts of distinct participation, they can yet come together until they merge. In other words to examine the reasons which ensure that the symbolic actions (stones which show the taro how to grow, etc. . . .) which are, beyond doubt, prefigurations which it is believed are capable of effectively producing what they represent, that is to say realize in advance, tend not to be distinguished from actions such as those of sympathetic magic (acting on the shadow or the appurtenances of an individual is to act on the individual himself) and can be, from a certain point of view, considered prefigurations. In fact, it is indeed in this way that they are considered by those who practise them and who do not doubt their efficacy.

In fact, for many anthropologists, the expressions sympathetic magic and magic or symbolic action are equivalent and are used indifferently. How is this to be reconciled with the distinction between two sorts of participation? If we manage to explain this we will have in the same breath a clearer view of this distinction and at the same time of what the two sorts of participation have in common.

September 7th, 1938.

Let us consider an action conditioned by a participation of the first sort: the Australian who strikes his spear into the imprint left by the kangaroo's foot, or the magician who has made a waxen image of his victim and pierces it. The end sought is certainly attained because there is community of essence, substantial participation between the footprint and the kangaroo, between the image and the victim. Consequently, since participation is independent of space, to wound the footprint is to wound *ipso facto* the kangaroo, to pierce the image is to pierce *ipso facto* the designated victim (whose name the image has been given). But one can say just as correctly that the action thus performed is an action through prefiguration. The Australian, in wounding the kangaroo's footprint, the magician, in piercing the victim's image, prefigure the result which they desire to obtain. Without doubt this result becomes already real by the sole fact of their act. But it has been seen (Volume VI) that in the thought of 'primitive men' the prefiguration is already the fact realized. In consequence these actions (and all those of the same type) which seem at first clearly related to participations of the first sort lend themselves equally well to the other interpretation. The magician prefigures the piercing of his victim; the Australian will prefigure the halting of the kangaroo's progress by the wound made in his footprint. If the native were able to grasp the difference between the two interpretations, and if he were invited to say which is his, he would certainly abstain from choosing and would give the answer which he believes to be most agreeable to the white man who asks him this singular question.

Let us now consider an action evidently conditioned by a participation of the second sort. In order to obtain an abundant paddy harvest, the Naga descend from their paddy fields with the back bent *as if they* were burdened under a load weighing on their shoulders. Or again the Papuans bury in their planta- tions stones of which the size and roundness are going to serve as models for the roots which grow. Or again, in order to make rain fall, the Australians imitate what happens when they are exposed to a downpour. These practices, and all those of the same type, make sense only if they bring true the desired result, and the natives believe that they *really* have this effect. Thus, for the Naga, the abundant harvest is not only prefigured (as we understand it, with the idea that prefiguration has, according to 'primitive men', the magical power of bringing about what it represents); it is already realized. We do not accept that because we do [not] understand how a harvest which will reach maturity only in three or four months' time can be abundant that very day when all the events which can happen in the interval and affect the harvest in one way or another are not known.

But the Naga do not need to understand. It is enough for them to feel that the prefiguration (imitation of the desired event) determines a participation. And as to the incompatibility of the present determination of the harvest's abundance with the fact that storms, devastations, etc., may occur before the date when the rice will in fact be ripe, that does not affect them either because it cannot be present in their mind: if imitation is truly participation (of which they have no doubt) the felt participation is independent of time as of space, and by virtue of this what will be real is so already.—Same interpretation for the Australians' mimicry when they act *as if* the downpour were soaking them: this is not a prefiguration of the rain; this imitation effectively *realizes* the rain which will fall soon, tonight or tomorrow; the imitation is a felt participation, and, as such, independent of time. The result is obtained and it little matters whether it is in the future (as the paddy harvest) since it is already real. In other words the felt participation is independent of time (like the series of secondary causes, cf. *Primitive Mentality*).—Finally, when the stones buried in the plantation 'teach' the roots the size and shape which they should attain, this imitation, which at one and the same time is suggested to them and imposed on them, is felt by the natives as a 'directed' participation which makes the desired qualities pass from the stones to the roots. Present in the stones, by the effect of participation these qualities are (through anticipation) in the roots: the participation is felt as in the prefiguration of the Nagas, and with the same indifference to the conditions of time.

If this is so, these actions by prefiguration clearly approximate those which are conditioned by participations of the first sort, and seem to require, as they do, a double interpretation. The magician, in piercing the image, effectively pierces his victim, or (second interpretation) prefigures this result in order to achieve it, and thus in effect achieves it. Likewise the mimicry of the Australians who act as if the downpour were falling prefigures the rain in order to obtain it (first interpretation) or, by virtue of imitation equalling participation, makes it really fall already. It is felt to be actually falling (second interpretation) as the magician feels that he pierces not simply the image but the very body of the victim. The result obtained is *at one and the same time* in the present and the future, and it has no need of direct verification by the senses. It is certain, by virtue of participation-imitation, that the rain will fall, a little sooner or a little later, but that is of no importance to the efficacy of the action performed. And if it does not fall (if the paddy harvest is mediocre, if the taros remain small, etc. . . .) that simply proves that a mystical action has occured to neutralize what has been done.

September 7th, 1938.

IMITATION EQUALS PARTICIPATION ($\mathrm{M}\iota\mu\eta\sigma\iota\varsigma=\mathrm{M}\epsilon\theta\epsilon\xi\iota\varsigma$)

Thanks to these characteristic modes of action which allow the mainsprings which put them in motion to be seen without possible ambiguity, we can clearly discern, beneath the differences between the two sorts of participation, what they have in common, which explains why they have the same name. Without doubt the first sort comprises the participations so to speak of essence, and the second the participations-imitations. But, at the same time, it is necessary to take account of two very important points, which conspicuously weaken the difference. First, participation-imitation involves something very different from a relation of reproduction to original, of portrait to model. It has a metaphysical significance: it does not express a relationship between given things and objects; it founds an existence (legitimation, as we have seen in so large a number of myths of the aetiological sort (Volume V)). Imitation ($\mu\iota\mu\eta\sigma\iota\varsigma$) is the *raison d'être*, not by way of causality but by way of consubstantiality, that is to say of essence, communicated and divided; in brief it is a true participation ($\mu\epsilon\theta\epsilon\xi\iota\varsigma$) and, from this point of view it is nearly no longer distinguishable from the first sort. To recall some examples: precedents, archetypal models, *raison d'être* of events, qualities, individuals.

September 8th, 1938.

It is possible to present this remark in a slightly different and simpler way. The numerous symbolic actions by prefiguration, and those, of very varied applications, which rest on the principle *similia similibus* are visibly closely copied from the participation-imitation type. By prefiguring the desired result, one will obtain it, or, better put, one obtains it already: it is already real. (Cf. the Eskimo formulae from Thalbilzer.) Between his mimicry, which imitates what happens when a downpour occurs and the real rainfall, the Australian does not conceive, however dimly, a relation of cause and effect: to be honest, he conceives nothing, properly speaking. But he feels that, from the act of his mimicry, the rain is already there, although he may not perceive it immediately; likewise the Naga, etc. . . . . This unanalysable feeling is the mechanism for all these actions by prefiguration. Thus, as they are modelled closely on participation-imitation, the latter must also be understood (to the extent that it can be) through this same unanalysable feeling of the participation ($\mu\acute{\epsilon}\theta\epsilon\xi\iota\varsigma$) between the precedent and the event which produces it, between the actual individual and his mythical prototype, between portrait and model, etc. . . . .

HOW A DUALITY-UNITY IS FELT

Second. The other, much more important point which is common to the two sorts of participation which we have distinguished, and which justifies giving them the same name, is their equal indifference to the determinations of time and space. In general, a participation is felt as real without the subject who feels it needing to have regard to the situation, in time and space, of what participates and what is participated in. It is easy to demonstrate this through examples of both sorts taken at random.

Take the participation between the Naga and the leopard so that everything which happens to the leopard *ipso facto* happens to the man, and the inverse (although, for obvious reasons, the Naga insist much less on this point than on the first). The leopard is in the jungle in the vicinity of the village; he leads his life there like the other leopards who have no other existence; he hunts and kills to eat, etc. . . . . There is no contact of any sort between him and the human individual of whom he is the leopard; perhaps they have never met; they live in different although neighbouring places. This does not prevent the participation between them being so close and so intimate that together they form a duality-unity, which is felt both as a unity and as a duality, simultaneously by the man concerned and by all the other inhabitants of the village, as is plain from Hutton's account. Likewise, if the leopard is wounded, the man is also at the same moment and in the same part of the body; if he is killed, the man equally dies, although it may happen that the man only dies some days after. This interval of time may be more or less long or non-existent. It seems that in [all] cases participation may be equally intimate (duality-unity).

Another, no less striking example: participation between the corpse and the newly deceased. Usually, for various pressing reasons (above all fear of defilement) it is necessary to remove the corpse very quickly (premature-Hongra burials). But it is not believed that this rapid disposal removes the ghost, which would indeed be very welcome, for usually there is fear of it. On the contrary, one is persuaded that during the first (3 or 4) days the deceased remains in the closest neighbourhood, and often one even has the actual experience of his presence (Volume VI). This spatial separation of corpse and deceased does not prevent there being felt between them the closest and most intimate participation, a veritable duality-unity, such that the corpse is treated as if it were effectively the deceased. At meal times it is served food and drink, a fire is made before the corpse in order that the deceased might not be cold; at the moment when the body is borne to the grave or funeral pyre, the dead man is given messages for other members of the clan whom he is going to meet in the other world (on the other side of the pearly gates), etc. . . . As it has often been remarked, participation is almost always more complex, and not simply a matter of a duality-unity. The deceased is in his tomb, but he is also in the land of the dead, and yet he has returned to earth in the form of one or many lion cubs, of a grandson, etc. This multi-presence in different places, very distant from each other, does not seem to embarrass the natives in the slightest, although it scandalizes us. Participation which makes felt as a unity an individuality which appears to us to be a multiplicity of distinct things could clearly not be taken for real, as it is, without complete indifference to the place occupied by these things in this world and in the other world.

September 9th, 1938.

Notebook VII

September–October 1938

This trait is easily found in the other forms of the first sort of participation (through community of essence, consubstantiality, etc. . . .): the separation in space of what participates and what is participated in does not affect the participation. For example, appurtenances. Whether hair, nail pairings, saliva, or shadow of the individual occupy their usual place or are detached from it, or are transported to as great a distance away as one likes, the participation is not modified, and the principle 'pars pro toto' applies equally in all cases.

Likewise the symbols which for 'primitive men' represent the invisible beings, not by convention but by a true participation, that is to say they are consubstantial, are themselves, in the literal sense of the word, are most often separated in the most complete way; the symbols being perceived by the senses, the invisible beings forming part of the super- or extra-natural world: this does not stop participation from being as intense as possible. (Recall what is said in Volume VI about stones which are the ancestors petrified (monoliths, etc.), the ancestors being found at the same time in the land of the dead.)

Finally, let us take some cases of participation where this trait of which we speak stands out with the greatest clarity in the 'primitive' societies like those of Australia, New Guinea, Africa south of the Sahara, etc. . . ., the participation of each individual with the mythic ancestors who belong to the supernatural world, and which is realized most completely at the time of initiation, entails a genuine community of essence, a consubstantiality which is felt as intensely real, although the ancestors belong to the supernatural world; the feeling of this participation, reinforced periodically at the time of ceremonies, never disappears, if not from the consciousness at least from the subconscious of each individual. This last could only happen if he were to lose all feeling of his own existence, that is to say if he were to cease, in effect, to exist. In fact, simply the idea of this participation rupturing fills him with terror (for example, if, having failed to receive indispensable last rites or for some completely different reason, he should find himself, once he has become a ghost, excluded from the community of his clan's deceased, excommunicated, deprived of the participations which give them life).

It is barely necessary to give proof that the participations of the second sort (participation-imitation) are independent of the conditions of time and space. It is enough to recall the functions of these participations in the power of the myths (legitimation of events, customs, etc.), by the fact that in the myths the same events have taken place, that these customs have been practised, invented and expressly instituted by the mythic ancestors, etc. . . . Now it is not enough to say that these precedents are separated in time from the events and institutions which actually exist thanks to their participation with them (which the ceremonies renew when required)—the mythic precedents are not antecedents in the time which is familiar to us; they have their own time which is not the time of natural phenomena. And yet the participation between these precedents and the actual reality is felt in the most vivid way. Likewise as far as space is concerned. Neither from the point of view of action, does participation-imitation (symbolic action, sympathetic or imitative magic) at all depend on conditions of time and space (sorcery at a distance and delayed).

Bois de Boulogne: September 11th, 1938.

CASES OF DAGOMBA AND KWOTTO

A really marvellous example of participation: the account of the Dagomban hunter (Cardinall, *Togoland*, p. 79). The animal, mortally wounded in the forest, and the young Bantu who dies at the same time in the subterranean city form only a single and the same being, since the wound through which the animal loses his blood at the same stroke causes the young man to lose his blood. The two beings (one on earth, the other under the earth) are indeed two, but nevertheless they form only one; it is in this that the participation (duality-unity) consists. For the Dagomba (as for the Bororo, Naga, etc. . . .) there is no problem here; there is nothing extraordinary about this participation; they have seen and heard cited a very large number of cases; this one raises no more questions than the others. As for us, we can only take it as a story: if the duality-unity of animal and man is seriously presented to us as real, we do not even consent to discuss it. Why?—Because we do not see *how* the animal in the forest can be at the same time the young man in the subterranean city. We would want to understand, or at least not find ourselves in the presence of two incompatible claims. The Dagomba 'feels' the participation to be real and does not question further.

September 28th, 1938.

Let us compare with the preceding case what Wilson-Haffenden says on the subject of owls among the Kwotto. They are feared because their 'body is one of the shapes that evil wizards or spirits like to assume'.[1] Consequently they are birds only in appearance: in reality the owl is a dangerous human being or a spirit. Accordingly it is necessary to guard against killing it, through fear of reprisals on the part of other witches and spirits—or else only kill one if there is certainty of not being seen, for example in the forest, and of burying it carefully. Cf. The Lengua, who abandon killing the missionary Grubb, as they were prepared to do, through fear of his vengeance after his death, and the conviction of the Abipone and other Indians that it is not possible to kill the *kanaima*-jaguars, and that one must not attack them. The *kanaima*-jaguar and the witch-owl are good examples of participation between two individuals, who, under their true aspect, form only one.

More characteristic still is the following belief, reported from the same place by Wilson-Haffenden. 'If an owl possessing the soul of a wizard were killed or wounded by a hunter, the wizard in question would simultaneously experience an analogous shock in the human body. Thus, when a man suspected of being a

[1] Wilson-Haffenden, J. R. 'Ethnological Notes on the Kwottos of Toto (Panda) District, Keffi Division, Benue Province, Northern Nigeria', *Journal of African Society* (Vol. XXVII, 1927/28, p. 26). [Translator's note]

wizard falls sick or dies, it is said, "Perhaps some brave hunter killed his owl counterpart secretly in the forest, and to him are we indebted for this happy deliverance."[1]

Accordingly the owl is not simply a form which the witch or the spirit takes at will, as the Abipone witch transforms himself into a jaguar, and others into a crocodile, snake, etc. . . . A particular owl is united to a particular witch in such a way that from what happens to the one which is seen it is possible to infer with certainty what has happened to the other, unseen one. This union which is independent of every condition of time and place goes beyond a bond of sympathy, as close as one likes. It deserves to be called participation, in as much as the two beings, each of whom seems to live their own life, nevertheless only live if the other continues to live, that is to say as if the two were only one. The duality and the unity are equally real. The witch dies, the owl *must* have been killed. Little matter that this participation is not explained.

September 30th, 1938.

PARTICIPATION, FLUIDITY, MYTHICAL DREAMS

A remark on the preceding sort of participation: the duality-unity of the witch-owl among the Kwotto, like that of the Naga-leopard, of the kanaima-jaguar and so many other similar cases, does not, for the primitive mentality, need explanation, because as soon as it is known that it is a question of a witch, the explanation is given in advance, *ipso facto* so to speak. As it is said in the French West African court proceedings witches can do everything, and so there is no need to seek how they may be at one and the same time a man in the village and an animal in the forest or the river: for them nothing is impossible. This belief has existed until the present in western Europe itself: were-wolves are witches in animal form, and maleficent witches have the power to take this form; seeing that they can do this, those who hold this belief do not dream of asking how the transformation is possible. This transformation or this duality is an unquestionable fact, and one looks no further.

Perhaps it is possible to generalize this view, which seems well

[1] Wilson-Haffenden, op. cit.

founded as far as the duality-unity of witches is concerned. Let us recall that the complex of beliefs, emotions and representations linked to witchcraft is closely attached to the complex which is connected with the mythical world. The world of witchcraft is fluid like that of myths: that is expressed, among other things, by the considerable importance which it gives to participation, that is to say to the connections or preconnections of things or phenomena independent of every physical condition of possibility. Now, in the case of participation where it is [not] a question of witchcraft, as, for example, in the Dagomba case, in the story of the king vultures (Koch-Grünberg), etc. . . ., it is striking that consideration of the possibility does not arise to a greater extent, either from a logical point of view or from a physical point of view. This makes us think that we are here in the presence of a reality similar to that in which witches operate, that is to say of a reality fluid like that of the mythical world, neither governed by laws nor fixed in forms (concepts). Accordingly, to feel participations between things and phenomena is to find oneself in the attitude familiar to the human mind when it feels itself in contact with the mythical world fluid reality, forces at one and the same time transcendent and immanent.

September 30th, 1938.

I fear that there might be something inexact and confusing in what precedes. Belief in the unlimited powers of witches is distinct from the belief in participation that I call duality-unity. We find these dualities-unities attested in a very large number of cases where there is no question of witchcraft at all. And, on the other hand, the Naga-leopard (cited in Volume IV) expressly says in his defence that, if he is a man leopard, it is not he who wished it, that it is not his fault, and that he ought not to be treated as if he were responsible. Also to remark that the people of the village complain of the damage caused by the leopard (who is also the man), but do not accuse the man of being a maleficent witch.

Accordingly to renounce the rapprochement indicated above. What may be kept is the general consideration which I wrongly based on this rapprochement, to know that participations felt and considered as real—for example the duality-unity in the

K

cases cited—do not absolutely depend on conditions of possibility, whether logical or physical, and that they thus place us in the presence of the same complex as the mythical world.

October 1st, 1938.

What I had not seen at all when I spoke of participation in *How Natives Think* is that it is closely linked to the representation of the mythical world and to the confidence which the primitive mentality has in the mystical experience. I had the preconceived idea, which has been shown to be wrong, that participation proceeds, if not from a peculiarity of logical thought in 'primitive peoples', at least from special habits of this thought different from ours; an idea which used to seem plausible and clear, but which was neither one thing nor the other.

Today, after Volumes V and VI and following the assembly and analysis of a large number of facts, I have given up this idea. I state simply that the minds which live in the milieu of participations, which treat them as real as the rest of their experience and would never have the idea of doubting them nor of asking themselves the least question as to their cause, are those same minds for which 1., the mythical world has been and still is real, with its perfect fluidity and the transformations of every sort which constantly take place there—and 2., the mythical experience, although felt as qualitatively distinct from the common experience, is nevertheless also a genuine experience to the same degree and intermingled with it in a way that they constitute together one and the same experience.

How to prove that the feeling of participation is solidary with the representation of the mythical world and with the confidence in the value of the mystical experience?—In many ways. In the first place, in noting that one of the essential characteristics of this representation and of this experience is that they are both independent of the conditions of time, space and causality to which common experience is necessarily submitted, or, in other words, from the point of view of this representation and this experience nothing is impossible *a priori*. No matter what happens, and since the most unbelievable event or transformation (according to us, and from the point of view of intelligibility) occurs, it was therefore possible. So there is no thought of doubting it. Now this characteristic, as we have seen above, also belongs to a large number of participations. The fact that we have not seen how a participation is reconciled with the conditions of time and place, nor how it can be conceived as physically possible does not question it. It is no less felt and considered as perfectly real. Why not acknowledge here the same orientation, the same mental disposition which makes the representation of the mythical world and the mystical experience accepted as real?

Now the most essential trait of this mental disposition—which, for greater clarity, can be defined by opposition to that which is most habitual for us—is that of not subjecting what is taken for real to any *a priori* condition of possibility. I had caught sight of this, and had concluded—wrongly, it seems—that these minds are more indifferent than ours to contradiction. In fact, there is no distinction to be made on this point between the primitive mentality and our own, if the word contradiction is taken in its strict sense. But they are not sensitive to incompatibilities (not prelogical, but physical) which we certainly do not tolerate. This I am now in a position to explain through the confidence which they have that the mystical experience is a genuine experience, and through the fact that the representation of the mythical world is not conceptual.

October 1938.

PARTICIPATION—EXPERIENCE OR BELIEF

2., If, as it seems, participation is not a constitutive element of the human mind of which the function would be to link in a certain way, in determined conditions the objects that it perceives and thinks, it would then be necessary for it to form part of the data of experience in the human mind. Is this so? And could this hypothesis be verified?

In the first place, if it is no longer a question of a sort of *a priori* element which would naturally apply itself in a similar way to all the objects to which it might apply itself, the inquiry ought to start with an effort to distinguish and classify, if it is possible, the various sorts of participation which the study of the primitive mentality has brought to light. It is clear, for example, that the participation between a person and his appurtenances is not identical to the participation between him and the other members of the social group to which he belongs (family, clan, phratry, tribe) or between him and his group's ancestors, whether of this world or the mythical world. The participation between the Naga and his leopard or between the Kwotto witch and his owl, etc. . . . is yet another sort. It might be important to make an exact account of these differences—and yet I have the very strong feeling that in these cases, so different, the essential element of the participation is the same: it is doubtless this feeling which urged me to see there an element peculiar to the mind which projected it onto its objects.

A certain number of questions immediately arise. But I will abstain from all dialectical discussion or research, and I will keep to the examination and analysis of concrete examples of different sorts of participation. For each sort the question to be resolved will be the following: if participation is given in the experience or with the experience how is this, and what sort of experience is concerned in this case?

An Australian woman believes herself lost because a lock of her hair is in the power of an individual from a neighbouring tribe, and it is the hardest thing in the world to pull her out of her despair. She is so persuaded that the participation between those hairs and her person is such that the possession of the hair is equivalent to possessing her person, that is to say that those hairs which are hers are she herself; an integral part of her individuality like her arms and legs, like her name and shadow, those hairs are this very individuality by virtue of the universally accepted principle: *Pars pro toto*. This is precisely the intimate participation, a sort of consubstantiality between the person and his appurtenances which makes this principle apply. The emotional state which disturbs the Australian woman allows no doubt about the force with which the participation is felt.

Is there an experience here? And of what sort? A white man witnessing the extraordinary distress of the Australian woman would doubtless say that it is not an experience. For he, if he knew that a lock of his hair is in the hands of his worst enemy would not be worried. He feels that his enemy has no means of making use of his hair in order to do him harm: he feels no participation between his person and the hairs which are no longer on his head. If participation were real, he would feel it.

Accordingly it is not an experience which throws the Australian woman into despair. It is only a belief, or, as the white man will say, a superstition analogous to so many others also relating to appurtenances. And if the Australian woman's circle of friends shares her terror, and would feel like her in the same circumstances, that does not mean that they have, at some time, the same experience, but that they have the same traditional beliefs and the same superstitions.

But I cannot stop myself from remembering here some penetrating reflections of Hallowell, cited in Volume VI. We have clear definitions of experience and belief which establish between them a distinction so powerful that confusion seems impossible. What is genuinely a datum of experience can be checked, verified, and in identical circumstances the experience is unfailingly the same for all human subjects (a sound, colour, shock, etc. . . .). How does it happen that the experience of those Australian Aborigines (participation of the individual with his cut hair) does not occur in white men?

One knows that this reasoning involves a definition of experience among us uncontested as a result of centuries of critical work, which has disqualified and excluded mystical experiences from valid experience. But, for those Australian Aborigines, as for the Saltaux and for so many others who have no idea of experience as it is defined in our societies, this definition is worthless. They constantly have mystical experiences which without the least hesitation and without a shadow of doubt crossing their minds, they recognize as having as much if not more value than ordinary experiences (cf. Volume VI); of course, it is not they who say this; it is evident from all their behaviour, individual and collective, and nothing could be more conclusive.

Of what therefore consists this Australian woman's experience, which according to us would not be one but which we do not have the right to deny in terms of a definition that does not perhaps embrace everything that there is to define? We understand the participation between a person and the hair on his head; we feel the participation, like the Australian woman, if someone pulls it rather roughly. If it is cut off, we no longer feel it; she still feels it—although she experiences no actual sensation, no matter what action is performed on it.

The observation is right; it is not as decisive as it seems to be at first because it does not take account of what the appurtenances are for those minds (refer back to the chapter in '*The 'Soul' of the Primitive*' where it is abundantly proved that the appurtenances of an individual *are* the individual himself); this 'extension' of the personality has as a direct consequence an extension of the experience. In the same way that the subject has the experience of his appurtenances which we also consider as such when it is a question of ourselves, he also has the experience of his other appurtenances which we do not consider as such. If he did not 'feel' this participation as a real experience, he would not say that these appurtenances are he himself.

But if the cut-off hair is pulled, if his excrement is burnt, etc., does he feel nothing?—Certainly, from the point of view that we call the positive experience. But, for him, his individuality, his personality is not limited to the periphery of his physical body: he has not even the idea of a purely material reality. His personality is everywhere he feels a participation with himself—and separation in space, as we know, constitutes no obstacle to the unity of the individual concerned.

October 2nd, 1938.

PROPER OBJECT OF THE WORK

The work about which I am thinking would not be a new book propounding a different though connected subject from the preceding volumes; it would be a bringing into sharper focus of a certain number of ideas and formulae which are to be found from beginning to end of the six volumes, but which I have developed (above all in the last three, but already a little before that) from 1910 to 1938, simultaneously through my own reflections and a sort of progressive self-criticism as the facts became better known to me and as I understood more their sense and significance—and also under the influence of the objections which were made, and of which I recognized those that seemed to me justified.

I do not believe that it would be interesting for the public to have a history, more or less detailed, of this evolution, especially as it is not entirely certain that the description which I would give of it would be sufficiently accurate. Others, more interested in the affair, would certainly see better what has happened, if they were to make the effort, whereas I would greatly risk falling more or less naively into the rather crudely set snares of vanity. With the best will in the world, one can never be certain of avoiding them, and the wisest thing is to speak about oneself as little as possible when one is not obliged to do so.

It seems to me that there would be an advantage for me in drawing up a provisional list of the statements and formulae on which this restatement should bear. *Im Werden*, a list which by nature remains open, where I can at any moment remove or add something, until I have the feeling that it is complete enough for me to take it as the outline of this work. The order which the questions are going to follow is not definite; it is purely arbitrary, and must give way to another, precisely based on the study of the topics, which will disengage the relations between them. In particular, this order must allow the greatest possible avoidance of repetitions from which a restatement can barely be entirely free, and to reduce to the smallest possible number references to passages from volumes which will be indispensable, and which always risk antagonizing the reader if he does not take the trouble to refer to the passages indicated.

October 8th, 1938.

CONTRADICTION? NO, BUT INCOMPATIBILITY

The first point to take up again—and one which controls many others—is the one that has earned me the largest number of objections and attacks, and above all the most obstinate ones, all the explanations which I have given over the last thirty years having served little purpose. It is the formal distinction between two mentalities, the primitive and ours, and the opposition which I have sought to establish between their essential characteristics. Even many of the minds tempted to accept, in detail, the interpretation that I propose for a certain number of facts, refuse to accept what they believe to be my essential thesis, formulated above.

To show (useless to do it here, even in summary) that I do not assert (today less than ever) that there exists a mentality peculiar to 'primitive peoples'. There is in their mentality a large part which they have in common with us. Equally, there is in the mentality of our societies a part (larger or small according to the general conditions, beliefs, institutions, social classes, etc. . . .) which is common to it and to that of 'primitive peoples'. For the convenience of exposition, it is possible to separate that part from the rest, and in order to describe it and analyse it more easily, to consider it by preference among 'savages' by letting it have the name primitive mentality,—it being understood of course that it is something human and which is not met exclusively in societies called primitive, and that it is also met in other societies.

Thus the fundamental misunderstanding is dissipated at once and my present position no longer involving ambiguity, like those to which certain unfortunate expressions in *How Natives Think* have given birth, I pass to other points bound up with the first.

2. In *How Natives Think* I determined two essential characteristics peculiar to this primitive mentality: mystical and prelogical, which furthermore I already felt to be closely linked to one another to the point of saying that this mentality is prelogical because it is mystical. But I had not elaborated this view; otherwise I would not have placed these two characteristics on the same level, nor have accorded them the same importance; if I had fully understood the nature of the mystical experience (which I have disengaged only slowly, mainly in Volumes V and VI) I would also have seen that from this mystical orientation of minds necessarily results what I then called, rather awkwardly, by the term prelogical.

3. Starting from there in order to rectify some formulae of which I made use in the first three volumes without having plumbed the sense which it was legitimate to give them:

(a). the primitive mentality is lesss sensitive than ours to contradiction; it does not expressly accept it, but tolerates it, etc. . . . To explain that on looking at it closer, it is not a question of contradiction in the rigorous sense of the word,—of incompatibility in the physical sense, but not of logical absurdity.

(b). 'it has not the same logical exigencies as ours' is a vague expression, as it is also when I wrote that 'their mental habits differ from ours'; if one wishes to define these expressions more carefully, they basically say the same thing as the preceding (a), and, as such, ought to be abandoned because, underlying, is found the idea that there is a real difference between those minds and ours from the point of view of the logical structure and functioning, which has been energetically contested by people who had lived with 'primitive peoples' and had observed them well—and rightly contested.

4. The primitive mentality is not conceptual. An impossible affirmation to maintain strictly, as I felt almost immediately, and said then, as early as *How Natives Think*, 'it is not conceptual like ours', but, except for some general considerations on abstraction, generalization and classification in the primitive mentality, I did not at the time seek to study thoroughly what are the concepts of the primitive mentality, in what and how they differ from our concepts. I have become only slowly aware of this very important problem, and only in the light of what I established in Volumes V and VI. It is closely connected to the preceding question; is there not something which distinguishes the primitive mentality from ours from the logical point of view? We are always tempted to believe so, even after it has been shown to us that they are similar to us in this regard. A fairly superficial study of their concepts and ours would doubtless show whence this feeling arises and whether it is justified.

October 12th, 1938.

THE PRIMITIVE MENTALITY AT ONE AND THE SAME TIME
CONCEPTUAL AND AFFECTIVE

When in *How Natives Think*, *Primitive Mentality* and even in *The 'Soul' of the Primitive*, I frequently used the expression: this mentality is not conceptual like ours, it remained vague and certainly did not mean that it does not form concepts. What I had imprecisely in mind was this: they do not make the same use as we do of discursive reason; they are not familiar with its operations; the slightest abstract reasoning tires them and becomes for them immediately harassing. Why? Because they do not have at their disposal the indispensable logical material which makes these operations simple and reasoning easy: they lack the hierarchies of concepts which allow the subsuming of some things under others, and by operating on the concepts to obtain without great difficulty results which are valid for objects.

Thus I was far from saying that they do not have concepts

but was insisting on the fact that they do not derive from the use of their concepts what we derive from the use of ours. I also had the idea (a little preconceived) that theirs remain much closer to the concrete, and more in the direct proximity of the experience of perceived and given objects and facts. They have names for the different varieties and sub-varieties of a plant which is of interest to them, and no name for the plant in general—for the different stretches of a river's course, its bends and turns, and none for the river itself, etc. . . . This fact is correct, although there are some exceptions of which it is necessary to take account. But I would no longer insist on this as much as I did, or, at least, I would no longer express it in the same way. It remains true that the most simple logical operations generally disconcert them, and worry them, but that does not mean to say that their thought is not conceptual.

On the contrary it is necessary to recognize that the primitive mentality is, if not entirely like ours, at least similar for the essential and decisive reason that they, like us, have language; in consequence, that they have at their disposal symbols which represent for them as for us collections of things and objects in which they have noted the common charcteristics, species, types, states, actions, etc. . . . (common nouns and verbs). Even in admitting that these 'primitive men's' thought is never far removed from concrete representations, the use of linguistic signs places them on a level completely different from that where they would operate if they had at their disposal only images, even composite ones. It is enough to regard the complexity of their languages, their way of telling their proverbs, the psychological shrewdness of which many are capable, etc. . . .

Not to exaggerate, however, their resemblance to us on this point. Doubtless they have concepts as we do and on a very large number of occasions the use to which they put them does not differ from ours. But in certain cases at least, the symbols which represent these concepts—words—differ from ours. For us the relation of words to the concepts which they express is arbitrary, and we even know, without having to reflect on it, that it is conventional: there is nothing in the word 'bread' of the nature of the food which it designates. Whereas, for the 'primitive man' words, those symbols, participate, like other symbols, in what they represent; they *are*, to a certain degree, what they express, and common nouns are felt, like proper nouns, as appurtenances of what they designate. To pronounce the name elephant or tiger, etc., is not simply to awake the idea in those who hear it, it is to evoke it, it is to make it present, in the full sense of the term; it is perhaps to disturb it, to offend it, to attract blunderingly its attention and its anger. In many societies it is necessary to guard against pronouncing the name of animals and birds which are to be hunted shortly. This would be equivalent, literally, to warning them, to putting them on their guard. The participation between the symbol and the things which it symbolizes produces its effect independently of every condition of distance.

Accordingly, for that mentality, there is an affective element inseparable from the symbol, and, as a consequence, from the concept which it represents, every time that it is a matter of a thing or a phenomenon of which the mystical qualities and properties make an impression on it. When this word is pronounced, when this concept, at the same moment, is presented to their mind, their attention is polarized more or less completely on these mystical qualities, and immediately their behaviour conforms to usages traditional in such cases: conditions clearly unfavourable for the logical operations of the mind preoccupied by other more urgent things. It is in this sense and in these cases that it is possible to say that their mentality is less conceptual than ours.

October 18th, 1938.

CONCEPTS AND THE STABILITY OF THE WORLD

This emotional element can act as a means of passing to a consideration where it is no longer a question of concepts in so far as they serve a logical function, but of the role which is assigned to them—at least to those which are related to the phenomena and other things of the surrounding milieu—in the structure of the world. From this point of view the difference between the role of concepts in the primitive mentality and their role in the structure of our world view (*Weltanschauung*) is striking. For us, these concepts express relations, combinations ruled by constant and necessary laws, and, if it is a matter of living things, animals or plants, forms no less regular and constant: concepts based on the comparison of things, the analysis and subordination of their characteristics, classifications equivalent to definitions.

Whence it follows that we consider it impossible for an organism to present characteristics incompatible with its definition, or its concept. The example of the Trumai: if the Trumai are men, they breathe with lungs; accordingly they cannot live at the bottom of the river; they would quickly be asphyxiated. Given the concept of man, it is impossible for him to be amphibious. That would be to affirm and deny the objective value of this concept at the same time. Would this be a contradiction as if one claimed that the square on the hypotenuse of a right-angled triangle is equal to the sum of the squares on the other two sides, or greater than it?

To return to the discussion above concerning the contradiction properly so called and examine the relations of logical contradiction and physical incompatibilities. Some experiences may be rejected, as excluded by the definition-concepts, but it also happens that some definition-concepts are modified when faced by certain experiences—which does not seem to apply to mathematical definitions. In any case, it is remarkable that in the primitive mentality, as accustomed to the mystical experience as to the other, these incompatibilities do not exist, or only rarely. In fact, in daily practice, the primitive mentality acts according to the belief that the laws of phenomena and the forms of living things are constant and it finds this to its advantage. But it equally accepts that there is nothing physically impossible, that is to say that no departure from this rule is excluded *a priori*. The objective value of the concepts does not exclude them from being confused.

October 19th, 1938.

Notebook VIII

October–November 1938

In the study of participation, I insist on the fact that the separation, the extension in space, even over a very great distance, do not appear to have any influence on it. A photograph transported to England can serve to bewitch the model still in Australia, etc. . . . Join to this the fact that action at a distance is considered completely natural! the *pointing of the bone* among the Australians, the Oba (manufactured snake which becomes alive) of the Marindanim (Wirz III, 69) and a lot of other similar cases (Bugiel).

To examine whether action at a distance is represented and felt according to the type of participation, or the inverse—and, in a more general way, whether participation which holds so large a place in the primitive mentality's representations is not linked by a close affinity to the habits and tendencies which have given birth to the representation of the mythical world—both being for the primordial condition the frequency of the mystical experience, the confidence of the primitive mentality in the objective value of this experience and the force of the emotional elements which are inseparable from it.

October 23rd, 1938.

An answer to the question posed on the preceding page: there is an element common to action at a distance (which is generally a magical operation or an act of witchcraft) and to participation, and one which can explain how both are accomplished without separation being the slightest obstacle. This element is also involved in the mystical experience which I recall on that same page, and is entirely characteristic of the primitive mentality's orientation. It consists of representing to itself or feeling (both at once in the majority of cases) that an effect is produced, or that something happens, without asking how this result is obtained or this phenomenon produced. The attention is exclusively concentrated, by a sort of emotional polarization at the start, on the realization, the appearance of the phenomenon or result, it being understood that the supernatural power in action has the ability to produce this phenomenon or that result. It does not imply the denial of a mechanism of secondary causes: on the contrary, the primitive mentality sees them very clearly; but it does not attach any importance to them.

October 24th, 1938.

This indifference to the chain of secondary causes which leads to a certain phenomenon, which, without it, would not take place according to us, explains a fact on which I have insisted since Volume IV, where I proposed an interpretation of it (the two Papuan witches and their rats). Have they created these rats for the purpose of gnawing the coconuts, have they simply ordered some rats who already exist or have they themselves taken the form of rats in order to achieve their goal? In the legend recorded by Landtman, it seems that it is a matter rather of rats made by the witches and given life: but the other hypotheses would fit just as well. For example the leopard which is in the service of the witch, or the witch himself who turns himself into a leopard for the occasion. The primitive mentality does not choose between the two ways of representing the process: for it, being interested only in the outcome, they are equivalent, or, if it is preferred, interchangeable: both equally answer the purpose. This is very clear in the French West African report where the unexpected death of a man bitten by a snake while leaving his plantation is attributed to a witch (divination by ordeal, process, etc.). The white men's inquiry seeks to make the witnesses say whether they have seen this snake, to make them describe it, whether they believe it to be an artificial snake, whether the witch himself acted or used an instrument (the snake). It is impossible to obtain any clear answer. The witnesses do not see the point of the question, have not asked themselves the question and do not see why the question might be of interest. Whatever way the witch worked, the result is the same and that alone is what matters. *We* consider secondary causes as efficient, and we thus preoccupy ourselves in determining the true chain of causes and effects which lead to a certain result. The primitive mentality, without ever having reflected on the problem of the causal nexus, feels the efficiency in the force (natural or supernatural) which generates the effect, the force alone is responsible and it alone needs to be examined: whence divination and ordeal, the only reasonable form of inquiry and investigation given the premises in the people's mind.

Here then is the reason for the indifference of the primitive mentality which does not see what interest there might be in determining the series of antecedents which result in some event, or, if it is preferred *how* the supernatural force in operation has proceeded, whether it has employed one or many instruments and, if it has, which.

Indifferent to positive conditions, the primitive mentality is therefore, in the same way, indifferent to the situation in space of things or objects concerned, and action at a distance does not appear to involve any difficulty for it. On the contrary and from what precedes, if the primitive mentality poses a question, it is not that of knowing how an action at a distance is practised, since, in its feeling and its belief, the supernatural powers do not have to take account of positive conditions of the appearance of phenomena. It is only later when attention is brought more and more to bear on the causal nexus and the regular sequence of phenomena that it is noticed that action at a distance was perhaps unintelligible. The primitive mentality not pursuing the intelligibility of the facts which strike it does not see the problem.

These considerations are valid for the mystical experience in general, and allow the resolution of the difficulty indicated above concerning participation. For the primitive mentality the latter occurs independently of spatial conditions. An individual who is in Rome is bewitched in France, and may die from a wound made in an image given his name. Since this mentality does not ask itself *how* the action performed is possible—all its attention being centred on the action itself which generates its effect directly, or at least, if it employs instruments has them submissively at its disposal, and is not the least troubled by obstacles or difficulties which the causal nexus of phenomena might oppose to it—no more does it ask itself *how* the action can be performed

at a distance. It is enough for it to be certain that the action is
really performed which implies that participation at a distance
is itself real.

October 25th, 1938.

FUNCTION OF CONCEPTS AND FLUIDITY

Another important consequence follows from what precedes.

When it is a matter of mystical experience or action, the
primitive mentality reveals itself indifferent to the causal nexus
of the phenomena involved in this experience or action, and we
have seen the reason for this. For the primitive mentality the
role of this nexus is secondary and subordinate, at the very most
it sees there an instrument, manageable and pliable at will, at the
service of the supernatural forces: these forces are the true causes,
and the sequences of phenomena may be modified, or substituted
for one another: the goal is no less achieved, if a superior supernatural force does not arise to paralyse what is being done. In
other words, as soon as it is a matter of mystical experience or
action, the consideration of the laws of nature fade into the
background; they are not denied, but in so far as they could
constitute an obstacle, they are put aside, and there is seen to
appear, in place of the determinism of phenomena which seems to
us the very framework of the ambient world, the characteristic
fluidity of the mythical world which is unaware of it.

Now in the world of living things, there is something which
corresponds to what are the laws of the physical world, constituting like them an essential element of permanency and fixity;
these are the forms of those things, which heredity transmits and
preserves so faithfully, and which are so peculiar to the innumerable species of plants and animals (to say nothing of crystals and
minerals) that they serve to define them and suffice to do so: where
would botany and zoology be without the classification that makes
the study of morphology possible?

Now, it is remarkable that, as soon as it is a matter of mystical
experience or action, the consideration of the specific forms fades
into the background as does that of the laws of physical phenomena. Again at this point, fluidity is substituted for constancy
and permanence. Just as the most unlikely events happen in the

mystical experience and just as magical operations produce results paradoxical, even absurd from the point of view of positive experience, likewise the most improbable transformations are accomplished without difficulty and many primitive men accept this not only for the mythical world in which they believe but also for the physical world in which they live, if for a moment they suspect there an intervention of the supernatural forces (cf. the French West African documents).

Thus it is that a penetrating observer like Im Thurn, and others as well have been able to say that for primitive men the form of things is only an accident (king vultures, deer, crocodiles, etc., which change form like clothing, animals which are not really so, shamans, witches who take *ad libitum* an animal form, etc.). *La Mythologie Primitive* and *L'Expérience Mystique* are full of facts that leave no room for doubt about this point.

If it is thus, we can give an entirely new exactness to the rather vague formula employed in *How Natives Think*: the primitive mentality is not conceptual like ours. It has been seen above how it is possible to obtain a closer grip on this thought by making a comparative study of the concepts peculiar to the primitive mentality and of those which are peculiar to our mentality, and of the use which can be made of both, of the widening utilization of the knowledge of nature's phenomena that the concepts allow or facilitate.

Thus what I used to consider in the concepts was more or less directly their psychological and above all their logical function. But now the forms of things being so to speak an aspect of their concept (γενος, idea, etc.), a deeper sense of the formula appears: the thought of primitive men is not conceptual like ours, that is important: neither the laws of nature nor the forms of living things play in their thought a role comparable with that which they do in our thought, at least as soon as it is a question of a mystical experience or a magical operation. Whereas for us concepts are rigid frameworks, where has to enter the reality perceived by us, which surrounds us and about which we must endeavour to know what is permanent in order that we may make ourselves as far as possible master of it, the concepts of the primitive mentality, like the forms which they express, offer no resistance to fluidity, as soon as it is a question of mystical experience.

October 25th, 1938.

L

Thus, to say that the thought of primitive men is barely conceptual is equivalent, in fact, to saying that it is not tied to the inviolability of the laws of phenomena nor to the permanency and constancy of the forms of organisms, or, in other words, is never embarrassed by what we would call miracles or ruptures in the natural order. In this way, this formula is allied to those discussed above (if the latter are also understood not as I formulated them thirty years ago but as I do today: those minds, in certain circumstances, tolerate much more readily than ours what is contradictory, have less demand of logical rigour, have other mental habits, etc.). I see today that it is not a matter of contradiction in the true sense of the word, but only of incompatibility with what we believe to be entirely certain from the point of view of experience, that it is a question not of logical but physical absurdities (the Trumai who sleep at night at the bottom of the river, etc.). For us, given that the Trumai are men, this is excluded, it is entirely impossible for them to pass their nights at the bottom of the river, and it is here that the difference in the role of concepts in those minds and in ours appears. Men are mammals, and as such they breathe through lungs, so it is impossible for them to stay under water for hours like fish and amphibians. Why impossible? Because according to us there is an incompatibility between the concept of man that involves a certain respiratory mechanism, and the prolonged stay in the water. It cannot be claimed at one and the same time that the Trumai are men and that they spend their nights at the bottom of the water: this is to affirm a concept and to deny it at one and the same time. If this is not a contradiction properly speaking, it is an intolerable incompatibility. Either it is untrue that the Trumai spend their nights at the bottom of the river, or they are not men. The force of the dilemma, which seems to us to admit of no discussion, arises from the concept man which has the value of a definition of a thing.

The attitude of the natives is very different. They start from what is for them a certain fact: the Trumai sleep at the bottom of the river; accordingly it is not impossible since it is done. For all that will the natives admit that the Trumai are not men, will they abandon the concept that seems to us incompatible with this fact?

An answer to a question which they are so very far from

asking themselves cannot reasonably be expected from them. But it is not rash to imagine the answer which they might give. Certainly the Trumai are men. But, although resulting in the extension of the concept man, experience proves that they possess a power that other men do not have: that of staying under the water without asphyxiating themselves. This property is not as paradoxical as it seems to us: there are other men, in every human group, who have in a like manner powers belonging only to themselves, physical privileges: the witch, the medicine man, the shaman who has the power to make himself invisible, to transform himself into such and such an animal, to exercise a magical action at a distance, etc. . . . The Eskimo shaman goes to the bottom of the ocean without risk of being drowned, likewise he goes to the moon. He is, however, a man, but one who, under certain circumstances, and through the fact of his initiation, is at the same time more than a man according to the expression used by the Australians for their medicine men. These minds do not abandon the concept of man—but for them it is supple and flexible, whereas for us it is rigid and fixed.

What has just been said about the concept man is valid for the other concepts of things and objects of nature. The incompatibilities which for us result from these concepts are not rejected by the primitive mentality; in the majority of cases it does not even notice them. Why this difference? Sufficient explanation is to be found, I believe, in Volumes V and VI. It is that for us what is contrary to well established, checked and verified positive experience has no objective value: it can only be dream, fiction, story or myth. And what this positive experience accepts and excludes is incorporated in the concepts. Whereas for the primitive mentality there exists alongside this experience or, better said, there coexists with it a mystical experience which has as much, if not more value than it, and which affirms the reality of these continual exceptions and infractions to the regular order of nature. The fluidity of the mythical world is no less real than the regularity of the laws and the constancy of the forms in the natural world.

Thus there is not, as I have believed and said for a long time, a character peculiar to the primitive mentality that consists of a difference between it and ours from a logical point of view: a certain tolerance of contradiction, lesser logical exigencies, etc.... More simply, there is a direct consequence of this mentality's mystical character, which is constantly expressed by its orientation (indifference to secondary causes which are never the true causes), by the uncontested value that it gives to dreams, and generally to the mystical experience, through the fact that for it myths are true stories, through its belief in the reality of the fluid mythical world, and through its confidence in modes of action based on these beliefs (participation-imitation, symbolic prefiguration, etc.).

If we are not fully awake to this mystical character of the primitive mentality and of its confidence in the mystical experience a lot of beliefs and ways of acting will appear absurd to us, and we will think that there is a difference between them and us from the logical point of view. But we now see that this hypothesis is gratuitous.

October 26th, 1938.

RELATION OF THE TWO EXPERIENCES FOR THE PRIMITIVE MENTALTY

On rereading in Notebook III the passage relating to the quotation from Einstein concerning the intelligibility of the world of sensible experience, I am led to give a better account of what this experience is for the primitive mentality. In order to make better understood what is for them the mystical experience and the mythical world I have insisted on the characteristics of this experience (for example, that of dreams, of the unusual, etc.) and on the 'fluidity' of the mystical world in striking opposition to the constancy of the laws and forms in the world of actual positive experience. But this opposition, striking for us, who see on one side the given reality, object of science, and on the other side stories, legends and myths without objective value, arbitrary like fiction, does not produce at all the same impression, does not take at all the same aspect in the eyes of primitive men; indeed they feel a difference between ordinary experience and mystical experience (affective category of the supernatural) but there is nevertheless for them only a single experience, in which the two experiences which we separate are the whole time mixed together: the mystical experience is for them at least as valid, as real as the other. The opposition is thus already found moderated and limited.

On the other hand they are not struck, as we are, by the fact that the world of verifiable experience is intelligible, whereas the mythical world is not. Because it is only for us in the great civilizations that have created the sciences and philosophies that the world of verifiable experience is, at least in part, intelligible. But the primitive man has not directed any effort of reflection in this direction. In practice, he anticipates regularity in the sequences of phenomena, and in general he is not disappointed, although when some extraordinary phenomena occur, he may be shocked: he immediately recognizes mystical experiences in them. When the regularity is maintained he profits by it, but without telling himself that it is founded on laws and involves an order which his intelligence could discover and analyse. He takes this regularity for granted, and it does not present to him an intelligibility greater than that of the fluidity of the mythical world. The latter, fluid, always confused by unforeseen events, is not intelligible, but it is no less felt as real. The world of ordinary experience, which almost always offers regular sequences and is equally felt as real, is no more intelligible: it is enough that regular sequences happen.

Thus, for those minds, there is no opposition, contrast, between these two worlds, arising from one being intelligible and the other not. Neither of them is intelligible to those minds, which do not worry about intelligibility: they have simply the feeling that there exists at one and the same time a natural world and a supernatural one without preoccupying themselves with *understanding* either of them; one is imposed on them, the other is revealed to them and they look no further.

I have been wrong in wanting to explain this difference between them and us on logical grounds. It arises from the fact that the mystical experience has for them an objective value which it does not have in our eyes (leaving aside miracles and religious faith). For them it is normal that the abnormal occurs, and their attention is focused on the consequences that affect them.

November 2nd, 1938.

MYTHS AND THE LAWS OF NATURE

The remarks that precede permit an answer to a question which inevitably comes to mind when I read *La Mythologie Primitive* and which I have not been able to refrain from asking, without yet having found a satisfactory solution. Do primitive men seriously take their myths for true histories? Do they think that the improbable facts, the instantaneous and inexplicable transformations of which the myths are full really happened? We try in vain, but we do not manage fully to believe it.

However, our doubt would lose much of its force if we did not lose from sight the fact that the world of ordinary experience is no more for them than it is for us. In practice, they behave as if they had complete confidence, equal to ours, in the constancy of the laws of nature and the permanency of forms of living beings: this is indeed necessary in order that they may survive, and their techniques bear witness to it. But at the same time, they have mystical experiences of which the impression on them is profound, which reveal to them the presence and action of supernatural and invisible forces that intervene at any moment in the regular course of natural phenomena: from this point of view, the difference between this world and the mystical world is only that of the greater to the smaller, and the facts recounted in myths are no longer incredible since they also happen in the actual reality: these events are simply much rarer in our time than they were in the mystical period. Generally women give birth to boys and girls. However, if a woman, for once in a while, was delivered of an animal: dog, crocodile, calf, or bird, the primitive man who learns of it will be surprised, probably frightened, but he will not refuse to believe it, or claim that the fact must be wrong because it is absurd and impossible.

In other words, for those minds the boundary between what is physically possible or impossible *in our world*, is not as clearly defined as it is for us; often even it is not defined at all, which I have expressed by saying that they barely have the sense of the impossible. A formula which is basically equivalent to saying that the laws which govern this world can be contradicted at any moment. Consequently, it becomes understandable that they genuinely take as true the histories recounted in the myths, since the principle of the constancy of laws and forms, which *a priori* prevents us from accepting them, is not imposed on them.

I now see clearly whence this difference arises: not from a different structure of the mind, nor even from different mental habits, nor from lesser logical exigencies. It is enough to understand well the mystical orientation of the primitive mentality, the value that the mystical experience has for it, the importance which the primitive mentality attaches to it, and the place which the affective category of the supernatural holds in it (insisting on 'affective'). Faith in the reality of the supernatural, the acceptance of the content of myths as true, follows directly from this.

The answer to the question asked above is thus as follows: we would be less surprised at the primitive mentality's attitude in the presence of the mystical world's improbabilities if we did not ascribe to it, without being aware of it, our own mental attitude in the presence of the actually existing world. Their attitude (practice apart) is very different: the required explanation is here.

November 3rd, 1938.

DUHAMEL DISCUSSION

Points to remember for the Duhamel discussion and perhaps also for the projected work.

1. Show that in order to treat of 'primitive cultures persisting in the modern world' there is no reason to make use of the evolutionist hypothesis, at least in its popular and simplistic form. Not to represent the primitive mentality as belonging to a phase which the civilizations traverse in order to pass through others successively and to reach the present phase which would be entirely distinct from the 'primitive'. This is a view of the mind which may please and flatter the imagination but does not seem founded on facts, nor able to agree with them.

However, there is no doubt that human societies evolve (and differently, it seems, from animals). Some civilizations are born, develop more or less quickly in various directions, attain a kind of apogee, decline more or less rapidly, and finally give way to others. It is the business of history to establish the facts as far as the documents allow and of sociology to study whether the facts obey the laws which we may be able to fix.

But, at the same time that we try thus to know the changes that human societies, from primitive civilizations to ours, have undergone and to explain them in a way satisfying to reason (effort to establish a sociological or anthropological theory)—we recognize that there is something which 'persists', which constitutes a sort of fixed element through the changes and succession of institutions. This is clear from the evidence of the remarks so often made on the subject of the mentality called primitive; but this mentality we constantly find around us, and even in us. There is no need to seek further to find in full vigour and flourishing the beliefs that seem most primitive or the mystical experiences which seem the most extraordinary (contact with the invisible reality, presence of supernatural forces, etc.). It used to be said that 'it resurges' always, that it represents something fundamental and indestructible in the nature of man (cf. the last chapter of *How Natives Think* where this indestructibility is already indicated, but little studied).

2. What would be necessary now is to examine this study in the light of what has been established in Volumes V and VI, that is to say what we have believed to discern on the subject of mystical experience and myths. I would ask the Duhamel question in the following terms: how does the mystical experience reveal itself in our civilizations and in what way does it differ from the mystical experience in primitive civilizations? and 3. the actual civilizations, the modern world, does it, like the primitive civilizations, give birth to and develop myths, and if yes (as it is possible to show without too much trouble) what is their role, function, power in comparison with primitive myths?

Thus I would not have to study the history of institutions in successive civilizations—an enormous task for which I am not at all prepared, but only to consider the institutions, customs and techniques in primitive civilizations on one hand and in the modern world on the other, and only to the extent that would be necessary in order to characterize properly the mystical experience and myths in both, that is to say to obtain the necessary facts.

October [November] 14th, 1938.

It immediately leaps to the eye that what persists through all changes and transformations, from the primitive civilizations until the modern world, what constitutes a sort of immutable and indelible base is that which is born of the physiological and psychological nature of man as it has been explained in Volume V on the subject of the basic conditions of the mystical experience (impression produced by isolation, fear of the unknown, revelation of a reality other than the ordinarily received reality: the affective category of the supernatural, etc.). Consequently one conceives that the *social* elements which enter into the mystical experience change progressively as the civilizations themselves are transformed, and the difference may become considerable; for example, the distance between the mystical experience of an Australian or an Eskimo and that of present day western man. But whatever this distance may be, the root remains the same: the affective category of the supernatural. Principal objective: to show how given this ever unchanging root the mystical experience (and the beliefs which are socially inseparable from it) takes new forms.

November 14th, 1938.

FOR THE BRÖNDAL ARTICLE

With a view to the article requested by Bröndal, reread in *How Natives Think* the part concerning numeration. I do not see anything important and truly new to add there. I can 1. insist on the affective character of 'primitive' numbers which in *How Natives Think* I called mystical, the number being represented separately as a number only progressively as this affective character weakened, and becoming truly what we call a number only when this character has entirely disappeared, or, in other words, the concept of number is perfectly abstract, having no longer anything affective about it: this implies that the number is entirely detached from the object numbered, and consequently will be indifferent and the same whatever this object may be. Now this perfect detachment, if it is not completely excluded when it is a matter of the primitive mentality, is surely very exceptional; it is more than rare that the primitive mentality's attention dwells on objects which leave it entirely indifferent. From this it is permissible to conclude that, without any doubt, primitive men like us are capable of counting, and that even

certain of them go fairly far in counting, but even in this case
the numbers which they use are not entirely similar to ours.

2. If we consider the procedures employed in order to count
(running over successively the fingers of one hand, the parts of
the body from the same side, followed by those from the other
side, etc.) or else numbered sets, which have each their name well
before the abstract numbers are named, we are led to believe that
numeration (or the operation employed in counting) among
primitive men is to begin with *visual*. Like sign language, it is
unworkable in the dark. This very obvious character tends to
disappear progressively as numbers receive names and as numeration is fitted into the uttered language caught by the ear. Little
by little each number becomes a concept more and more homogeneous with the others which precede it or follow it in the series,
and numeration becomes abstract by losing its visual conditions.
As proof of these reflections, let us cite the numeration characteristics of the Bergdama, and the fact that they remain attached
to it for reasons of habit and convenience, although around them
is used a numeration far more manageable and less cumbersome.

3. To pass from the consideration of numbered sets and of the
visual character of counting operations to the formula that I
have often used: one is not a number. It has an appearance of
paradox; it is necessary to qualify it and say: among primitive
peoples one is not a number like the other numbers. At first,
from the visual point of view, number-sets start only when at
least two things or objects are perceived, felt or thought of in one
understanding. A unique thing or object can only determine the
affirmation that it is single, and primitive languages in effect often
have a word to say not one, but a single one. Afterwards to cite
the cases where numeration is seen to begin not at one, but at two.
Finally, it is remarkable that in the Malayo-Polynesian societies
of the Island of Pâques, Madagascar, the word for two, *ma, lua,*
etc., and for five: *lima, rima,* etc., are constant, whereas the word
for one is not so at all, but extremely variable. As long as the
operations of counting remain visual, number one lives in the
shade; with the progress of abstraction and the formation of
numbers properly so called, the number one takes its place.

December 1st, 1938.

'PARS PRO TOTO' APPURTENANCES, PARTICIPATION

In regarding more closely the use (very often it is possible to say constant use) that 'primitive men' make of the principle *pars pro toto*, I am led to wonder whether I do not make a mistake in accepting, without previous examination, that it means for them the same thing as it does for us. For us, it always implies something quantitative. The whole is composed of it parts, the part is smaller than the whole; the part represents the whole, because the presence of the other parts necessary to complete it is understood, etc. . . . This quantitative fashion of conceiving the relation of the whole and the parts is strange to the primitive mentality. It supposes a certain detachment with regard to the considered whole, which is regarded simply as an indifferent object. It does not entail an affective element nor a feeling about the intimate relation between the whole and the parts.

On the contrary, when primitive man, either in his works of art or his modes of action, applies the principle *pars pro toto*, the relation of the part which in his eyes is equivalent to the whole is similar to that of the appurtenance to the thing with which it is consubstantial. The part is not less than the whole, nor felt and apprehended as a fragment of the whole; it *is* the whole itself, which is apprehended in it—as the hair, nails, etc., the image or the name of a person *are* that person himself. An eye on a shape without mouth and sometimes without nose is enough for this shape to be a face. A lower jaw *is* the skull of which it formed part, and this skull *is* the person whose brain it contained, etc.— In brief, what the part means for us is that other elements must be added to it in order to constitute the whole. What the part means for the primitive mentality is that it is the whole, the thing itself, which is felt and apprehended in it as it is in the appurtenances. The quantitative point of view is neglected; what interests the primitive mentality is the consubstantiality that ensures that the thing *is* in what we call its parts. This sense of the word 'to be', almost impossible to define rigorously, is clarified up to a certain point by participation. *Pars pro toto* must be interpreted in the same way.

December 1st, 1938.

Notebook IX
December 1938

TRUE MYTH HISTORIES. IN WHAT SENSE?

I have often insisted on the point that, improbable as it may seem to us, among 'primitive peoples' myths are taken as true histories. I have tried to show the reasons for this, and I believe these reasons to be still valid. But I have failed to ask myself if 'true' has the same sense for the 'primitive man' as for us.

I did not ask the question because it seemed clear that for them as for us true history means the account of one or many events which in actual fact happened, which have been real. Those events which myths relate are considered real, and that is why myths are 'true histories'.

But what I did not notice until now, and what has some important consequences, is that the word real has only one sense for us, and for the primitive man it has two. Real for us is unequivocal: that is real whose actual existence can be perceived or, directly or indirectly, proved uncontestably. What does not satisfy these conditions may be more or less probable, but cannot be part of reality. This conviction is integral to our idea of experience, to our idea of truth (or concrete reality).

Now the primitive mentality has not at all the same idea of experience. It is wider than ours. It will include, besides the ordinary experience which is like ours, the mystical experience which puts 'primitive man' in contact with another reality, revealed by that experience itself, and he does not dream of doubting it any more than the experience furnished by the impressions coming from the surrounding milieu. Thus, in his terms, real is not unequivocal, no more than 'experience', but just as the two experiences form only one for him so the two realities, although their difference may be clearly felt, form for him only a single reality, and reality, like experience, is bi-univocal.

147

We now discern the unperceived ambiguity that hinders us in the formula: 'for primitive men' myths are true histories, the events they relate are real. Yes, but real in the sense of the reality revealed by the mystical experience and not in the sense of the only reality true for us, that which is perceived or adequately proved. It follows that the difficulty is resolved. A myth is a true history. For the Marindanim, the history of Piekor really happened. But that is not wishing to say that for them it is an event as true as the flooding of the river which they observed yesterday, nor that they believe it in the same way. The history of Piekor is a myth. It forms part of the totality of events of the mythical world as the flood forms part of the totality of phenomena of the world perceived by the senses. The idea of asking themselves whether such or such a mythical event is real does not occur to them, since in advance and so to speak *a priori* the totality of the mythical world is real for them, just as the mystical experience is as valid if not more so than the other. Thus there is no reason for asking how it is that they accept as real such and such a mythical event, which is clearly absurd and impossible in our eyes. The only question would be: how do they accept that the mythical world is at least as real, though different, as the actual world?—To which question I have tried to reply in *Primitive Mentality*: the mythical world has its own time and space, etc. . . .

December 4th, 1938.

This analysis would appear adequate if the mythical world and the other world were clearly distinct and constituted kinds of independent universes, so that an event in one cannot be confused with an event in the other. But we know that this is not so, and that 'true' histories in the sense of the actual reality are very similar to mythical histories (Trumai, the woman-hyena of the Togo, etc.).

Therefore it is necessary, having distinguished the two 'realities' accepted by the primitive mentality, to unite them to each other and to understand that, for this thought which is not conceptual, these two realities, although felt as different, form however only a single reality, just as ordinary experience and mystical experience although felt as different yet form only a single experience. Then other problems appear: how can improbable events, from the order of the mythical reality, be taken as facts in the actual surrounding reality? Examine them as relations between belief and experience?

December 4th, 1938.

THE MEANING OF 'REALITY' FOR THE PRIMITIVE MENTALITY

A doubt analogous to the preceding one leads me to ask myself what the reality (of things or events) is for the primitive mentality and whether the word (accepting that they use it) has the same sense for them as for us, or at least if they represent this 'reality' as we do. The answer to this question is not simple. It seems certain that they distinguish, as we do, the stories invented ad lib to amuse children, and also grown-ups, and which are not taken as 'true histories', from legends which genuinely take the place of history, and myths which correspond well enough to our sacred writings, and which no one would ever dream of doubting.

The content of these myths, on which no doubt falls, is therefore real; but is it so entirely in the same sense as, for example, the content of daily experience or the history of last year is for us?—To this question it is difficult to give a firm and categorical answer, and one that is valid for all cases. The answer should specify at the outset whether, in each concrete case, it is a matter of a reality belonging to the surrounding world or to the mythical world. In this last case, it is necessary to understand that 'reality' is not connected to begin with, as it is for us, with the cognitive aspect of the complex in question, but in the first place with the affective aspect (which does not exclude the complex from containing some elements of representation, but they are subordinate). Strange though it may appear, there is a certain emotional tonality peculiar to the mystical experience, or to the representation of the myth, that constitutes the primordial and essential element of the 'reality' of that experience or the content of that myth. It is this that I wished to have understood when speaking (in Volume III) of the affective category of the supernatural, although then I had a less precise idea of it than I have today—and when I explained that the mystical experience reveals the presence, action or contact of the invisible or mythical reality, but without otherwise making itself known. And yet what is thus revealed is as real as that which is 'known'. It is for these reasons that, when speaking of the realities of the mystical experience or the mythical world, I habitually say that they are apprehended and felt, rather than known, by the primitive mentality. And two important consequences to remember appear.

1. As the mystical experience has no domain entirely distinct from that of the other experience since the two are mixed together and form only a single experience, and as, likewise, the events of the surrounding world can be connected as much as one likes with those of the mythical world, it follows that the preceding considerations are valid not only for the realities revealed by the mystical experience or represented in myths, but also, in a large number of cases, for the realities of the surrounding world. Whence this facility, so disconcerting for us, of accepting improbable, absurd and clearly impossible realities: it is necessary to understand that they are not properly known (inserted in an order of coherent concepts and compatible with each other) but 'apprehended' and 'felt' as themselves, independently of every relation with other known realities.

2. In other words, we find here the new position of the problem of the relations of belief and experience, and the necessity of understanding these relations in a manner different from that which our psychology and philosophy have done until now. For instance the ghost-shark of the Kanaka in Leenhardt: we will say that this is an 'experience' of that Kanaka yet that this experience in order to occur presupposes a collection of traditional beliefs which exist in him. Indeed the revelation here is the apprehension of a felt reality (characteristic deep emotion). The history of Piekor, on the contrary, seems to us like a 'belief' in a series of events of which the reality is also revealed, but not as an actually revealed experience. Between these two revelations: revelation-experience and revelation-belief, the primitive mentality experiences an extreme diversity of intermediary forms of revelation, of which it is very difficult to say whether they are closer to one or the other.

December 5th, 1938.

EXPERIENCE AND BELIEF

Now let us return to the facts from Hallowell and to the explanation that he gives of them (Volume VI). It seems to me that I
can now go a little further. To classify the facts differently,
according to their own characteristics, and not to force them into
the traditional frameworks of our psychology and our theory of
cognition (*Erkenntnistheorie*).

We will leave aside the facts of experience that are similar in
the primitive mentality and in our mentality: perceptions of the
senses, knowledge of the surrounding world and the regular
sequences of phenomena, etc. . . . There remain the mystical
experiences (those that are wholly so or in part) and the content of
myths, taken as true. In order to explain these, no longer will we
appeal to the familiar concepts of experience or belief, and in order
to understand Hallowell's facts, for example (a bear that understands speech, etc.) and a quantity of others of the same type that
I have cited, no longer will we ask if there are here experiences or
beliefs, and where the latter stops and the former starts, etc. . . .

Let us recognize that the problems thus posed are artificial,
and as a result do not admit of solutions, or that the solutions are
artificial like the problems. Let us make the point that it is not a
question of an essentially cognitive process (that is implicity
accepted by asking the question in terms of experience or belief,
which belong, since Plato, to the domain of the theory of cognition
(*Erkenntnistheorie*)) but of a process of apprehension of essentially
affective realities. This process is released by a revelation where
this reality occurs, and that is to say apprehended and felt owing
to the fact that an emotion *sui generis* is experienced (affective
category of the supernatural). There are grounds for distinguishing many forms of this revelation: revelation-experience (shark
of the Kanaka, *measa* cases, bewitchments, etc.), revelation-
tradition (myths, etc.). The difference between these forms seems
to us to be considerable, and we should try to discover in them
the familiar difference between experience and belief. But the
primitive mentality is differently oriented, and above all is sensitive to the mystical and affective character common to all these
revelations. Proof, the intimate kinship of the dream (mystical

M

experience) and the myth (revelation-tradition) which is natural
according to them but mysterious for us.

December 5th, 1938.

DREAM AND MYTH

Why is the intimate kinship between dream and myth, if obvious
to the Australians and the Indians of California, mysterious for
us? Because we have great difficulty in regarding myth in the
same light as they do and in understanding the emotions that it
arouses in them. We do not see, and above all do not feel the
revelation that it provides. For the dream it is different. There
are still, even in our societies, many people who feel that a dream
opens for them a view of what is hidden and gives them access
to a reality different from that of the surrounding world, in
brief, it is a revelation that touches them and sometimes troubles
them deeply. But the myths of 'primitive peoples' no longer have
for us an effect of this type. They are particularly strange, if not
to say absurd and incomprehensible, accounts; the heroes of
them are at least bizarre, and we do not feel ourselves to have
anything in common with them; in brief, we need to make an
effort in order to take an interest in them (even from the scholar's
detached point of view) and in order to understand what they
mean for the natives. Thus, let us make clear what is involved in
the idea that they are their sacred stories.

December 6th, 1938.

It is useless to treat of this last point here. I have done it
adequately, I believe, in Volume V. What it is not useless to
recall is that, given the idea and the feeling that these Australians
have of themselves, of the group of which they are the members,
of their relations with the ancestors in the mythical world,
eternal beings, creators, founders of institutions, ceremonies,
etc. . . ., nothing could be more important, nor more moving for
them than contact with these individuals from the mythical period
in which their own existence is founded. Now this is the contact
that the myth procures for them. Thence the incomparable
interest in these accounts that, for us, are only stories, but which
for the Australian are something completely different, and which

affect him in that which he holds the most intimate, the most secret, and the most dear, in his participation in the world of invisible reality, the myth makes exist. So in this sense, the myth is a revelation (and a contact) like the dream: a revelation expected, foreseen, known in advance, but nevertheless a revelation. Here, neither 'belief' nor 'experience' are adequate expressions: revelation and contact are better.

December 7th, 1938.

VARIOUS SORTS OF PARTICIPATION

In order to try to clarify participation, as far as possible, it seems necessary not to consider it in *globo* without distinction, but to study separately the various participations that we note in the experience of the primitive mentality. For example, it is impossible to regard the participation between an individual and his appurtenances as perfectly similar to the participation between the Naga and his leopard, and the latter as perfectly similar to the participation between the individual, his social group, the territory he inhabits, his mythical ancestors and others, etc. . . .

I don't believe there to be an advantage in seeking to establish from the outset a classification, or at least an exhaustive list, of these different sorts of participation-actions: I fear that it may comprise something forced and artificial and I prefer, conforming to my usual method, to take as many facts as possible and allow myself to be guided by them: the list will thus establish itself and without any pretension to being complete: there might remain sorts of participation of which I have not spoken, but even so doubtless these others could be compared with those that I have envisaged; it will be possible to determine up to what point they are related.

1. As far as the participation between a man or [and?] an animal, or even an object and its appurtenances is concerned one errs if one seeks to 'understand' the consubstantiality that seems involved in this participation, and to find in what sense 'primitive men' take the word 'to be' here. The hair, nails, excrement, footprints of a man are he himself. If he is dead and far-away, some of his appurtenances will represent him, that is to say they will assure his presence and the funerary honours will be

paid to them as though to his body itself. Lacking these, the clothes worn by him will do. There is something here which disconcerts us. We accept that the Australian woman believes that he who holds a lock of her hair has her in his power; it is not incomprehensible that the individual thus feels himself intimately connected with his hair as we feel ourselves present in our arms, legs and eyes which are indeed effectively us. But how is it possible to have the same representation in the case of footprints, or of clothing to which are paid the funerary rites as though to the person himself? How can the Bantu think that this clothing *is* the member of his group who is dead and far-away, and for whom it is absolutely necessary to assure the well-being in the other world by the completion of the obligatory ceremonies?

My answer is: he cannot. What causes the confusion is that we want to find an intelligible sense for the verb *to be* in this circumstance; we suppose that the participation here involves a definite act of understanding. In truth the participation is felt; if in the complex that occurs the representational elements are not excluded at least they do not hold the attention, and the latter, amenable to the actions of the emotional elements that occupy the consciousness, focuses entirely on what is felt in order to know exactly the participation. Participation is not felt between the footprints and the animal because the Australian thinks, judges that these traces are the animal. But, on the contrary, he acts on these footprints as on the animal itself because he feels the participation between the appurtenance and it.

In other words, when we try to understand participation of this sort, that is to say make it intelligible, to grasp how primitive man represents the appurtenance as equivalent to the animal, we arbitrarily pose a pseudo-problem, failing to consider this participation from the sole point of view that is right, that is to say first and foremost and above all as something affective and not representational. If we pose the problem as we should, we no longer ask ourselves what sense the 'primitive man' here gives to the verb to be, how the clothing is consubstantial with him who has impregnated it with his sweat, and may take his place in case of necessity. There remains to find out how far we can clarify what this sort of participation is by starting from the establishment of its affective character.

December 27th, 1938.

'PARS PRO TOTO': FELT PARTICIPATION

If what preceded is right, there are grounds for modifying and completing the interpretation given above of *pars pro toto*, and this interpretation will in its turn throw some light on what participation by appurtenance is.

When we see primitive man represent a face by an eye, a body by the skull or a jaw bone, a person by his hair, image or name, we believe that we discern there a direct application of *pars pro toto*. Doubtless, as I have said, the primitive mentality does not pay attention at all to the quantitative aspect of the relation of parts or of a part to the whole: on the contrary, it is a qualitative relationship which is imposed by it and which is *felt*. The skull, part of the body, evokes the whole of the body of which it forms part, and as a result the image or possession of this part is equivalent to the image or possession of the whole: and likewise for the other appurtenances, likewise for the relation of the eye to the complete face. It seems then that the participation between the individual and the appurtenances may be of the same nature as the equivalence of the part to the whole, and that this participation and this equivalence mutually illuminate each other.

Without contesting the interest of these considerations, which I myself have asserted, it is however necessary to recognize that there are some cases where they do not apply, and where the association is found to be missing. For certain appurtenances, where the participation with the individual is as close as that of other appurtenances, the idea would not occur of invoking a relation similar to that of *pars pro toto*. For example, the footprints are in no way a 'part' of the man or animal of which they are an appurtenance, although they *may be* him since to act on them is to act on him. Likewise the spear handle wielded by the warrior, the clothing of the dead Bantu far-away from his social group, etc. . . . It seems that in these cases, as in others similar, participation may be of the type that I tried to explain when speaking about 'primitive men's' symbols—that is to say the suggestion—affective—of the presence of the object or thing symbolized, through the feeling of a consubstantiality felt between the symbol and what is represented. It is from this point of view that footprints, the spear handle, the clothing, etc., are appurtenances of which the *felt* participation with the thing or object allows the actions that often astonish us. In them and through them, the presence of the thing or object is suggested and felt as real.

Then it can be asked whether these cases which do not come under the formula *pars pro toto* do not lead us to a more exact interpretation of this formula, of which primitive men make so constant and sometimes for us so surprising a use in practical matters and in art. Is it certain that it is for them a question of the principle of *pars pro toto* as we understand it? It is we who, very naturally as it seems to us, take the skull for part of the skeleton, the eye or nose for part of the face, etc., because with our habits of lucid thought we grasp, almost instinctively, the relation of a part to a clearly defined whole, and the equivalence of the complete sum of the parts with the whole considered as a known totality. But have we the certainty that 'primitive men' have this same mental habit? On reflection, it is neither proved, nor certain, nor is it even probable that for primitive man the skull, or the lower jaw is a 'part' of the body, the eye or the nose a 'part' of the face. Doubtless if the question were asked him, and if he were to understand it, he would reply that in effect they are 'parts'. But what I am calling attention to here is that his mind does not spontaneously dwell on these ideas of whole, parts and their relationships. He has no interest in this quantitative aspect. What concerns him and holds him is the quality through which the appurtenance is felt as being the thing or object itself, that is to say the participation between it and him.

Thus this participation does not make itself felt as the representation of an identity, or at least of a consubstantiality between the part and the whole; but what we call 'part' fulfils the essential function of the symbol (in the sense explained in Volume VI), that is to say to suggest and truly to assure the presence of the symbolized, since, thanks to this symbol, it is felt as real.

This interpretation of *pars pro toto* as used by 'primitive men' (skull not part but symbol of the skeleton and thus of the body, eye or nose not part but symbol of the face, etc.) has the advantage of being equally applicable to the appurtenances for which the principle of *pars pro toto* is irrelevant. The footprints are not a part of the man; but they are a symbol (in the sense recalled above) and thus imply a participation which allows an understanding of their role as an appurtenance. Likewise for the spear handle, the clothing soaked in sweat, and for the other symbols which we sometimes have difficulty in considering as appurtenances: a man's house, his canoe, etc. . . .

The conclusion at which we arrive concerning participations between objects or individuals and their appurtenances is as follows: they are not based on perceived relationships, be they as evident as those of the part with the whole, but rather on the *feeling* of the true presence of the individual or object, directly suggested by the presence of the appurtenance. And this feeling has no need of legitimation other than the very fact that it is felt.

December 27th, 1938.

PARTICIPATION FELT NOT THOUGHT

This conclusion only makes complete sense if, at the same time, one bears in mind the remarks made more than once above on the subject of the vocabulary that we are obliged to use for the description and analysis of the primitive mentality's processes. This vocabulary is completely inadequate and the whole time risks misrepresenting these processes. It has been constructed by psychologists, philosophers and logicians schooled in Aristotelian doctrine and is virtually useless for the study of processes that are far from being like those which Aristotle proposed as objects of study. For example, we have just seen that in order to understand the use made by primitive men of *pars pro toto* it was necessary to be very careful not to suppose that they have like us the concepts of whole and part and that they consider the relations between them as we do. The same precautions have to be taken for the terms symbol, and appurtenances, etc. . . .

The basic reason for the inadequacy of the terms for what needs to be expressed is this: we are accustomed to regard the mental process concerned—in particular, participations between things, objects, their appurtenances, etc.—as dependent on the intellect, as involving a mental activity, in discerning objects and the relations between them. And yet we are led to state that participations through appurtenances cannot be elucidated in a satisfactory way.

Why? Because, for the primitive mentality, there is no question here of intellectual operations, but of something apprehended as felt. In Deschamps' opinion, in his study of the Autaisaka, this mentality is essentially affective and active in these circumstances. An emotional complex occurs, a motor reaction follows immediately.

Thus, in the participations through appurtenances studied earlier what the primitive man apprehends is a presence which, although invisible, affects him (the Bantu's clothing, the Australian woman's hair, the spear handle): the dead man is felt as present through his clothing, the Australian woman feels herself present in the lock of her hair, etc.; the man, the clothing, the hair, etc., are represented, of course, but what is not represented is the participation that ensures, in a manner that the primitive man does not dream of trying to understand, that the man is present when the clothing is, etc.... We say that the clothing is the representative or the symbol,—yes, but on condition that we remind ourselves that these terms are not used by 'primitive men' nor any terms which correspond to them: for them the presence is felt.

If this is so, it is not possible to refrain from remarking that when the affective category of the supernatural comes into action there is also a presence revealed, a revelation accompanied by an emotion which the primitive man does not mistake. In the case of participations through appurtenances, there is no more or less sudden and startling revelation. But the affective character, the emotional element, is there, and there is also a presence which is apprehended, felt as objectively real, although not perceived. Is there something to conclude from this? This is to be examined.

December 28th, 1938.

If, in order to describe and analyse participation through appurtenances, it is necessary to avoid terms that imply an intellectual operation (such as thinking, representing, etc.) it is no more entirely satisfactory to use, as I have done, the following: apprehension through feeling; participation is not represented but felt; a process or complex essentially affective or emotional. In fact, the word to feel, in the use I make of it here, has a well defined sense only through opposition to 'perceive, represent', affective only through opposition to cognitive. However hard we try, we cannot make clear what these terms connote for us if this opposition is entirely excluded; we cannot be certain that this opposition may not be given with the terms, so to speak, may not be for us an integral element of their sense.

Now nothing proves that the primitive mentality knows this opposition, and it seems more than probable that it has never been aware of it. Consequently, when we say that the primitive mentality feels, and does not represent participation through appurtenances, we make use of a distinction which does not apply, and what happens has doubtlessly an affective character but one that we do not describe exactly.

December 28th, 1938.

DUHAMEL DISCUSSION

Two developments that might be included in the wireless talk on January 25th and might interest the public. 1. An introduction to the prejudices that so often arise when it is a matter of comparing primitive civilizations with our own. The tendency to consider as absurd or grotesque, or in any case as inferior what goes against our customs, and more particularly the prejudice spread by the evolutionist theory that was so popular in the second half of the nineteenth century—a success that has faded quickly enough but that has left some traces and just among those who were the first to study primitive civilizations systematically: Tylor, his numerous pupils and successors, Sir James and many others are in agreement that, like Herbert Spencer's evolutionism, evolution starts from the simple and progresses toward the complex, from the inorganic toward organization. Therefore primitive civilizations are simple in comparison with modern ones. Contradicted by the facts if one does not restrict oneself to appearances (languages, secret life of the Australians, etc.). A whole aspect of the life of these societies, and the most important in their eyes, necessarily escapes the observers who only pass through or remain a short time—and also the people (missionaries, administrators) who live there many years—so secret is it. Today researchers trained in good methods penetrate deeply and more surely.

2. What continues to exist of primitive men in the modern world. In every case there is a witness, as moraines are the

unchallengeable witnesses to a glacial period: it is folklore, where primitive men's ways of thinking and feeling are fully expressed, where it is easy to distinguish how the primitive mentality is opposed to ours on a wealth of points: (the world where nothing is impossible, fluidity—non-conceptual thought, indifference to secondary causes, etc.). Now these incompatible stories with their minimum of probability have been maintained across the centuries, and children are not alone in finding pleasure in them, so it must be that this mentality is simply repressed in us. This recognized it is easy to point out other traces in us (myths).

January 1st, 1939.

INDIVIDUAL AND GROUP: PARTICIPATION

Following the study of participation through appurtenances, it seems natural to pass to that of participation which might be called essential: the participation between the individual and a social group.

But here an unexpected difficulty arises. We have no need to look for a particular explanation of this participation; we are used to accepting it; we consider it as reasonable. The idea of the individual's solidarity with the group or groups to which he belongs is familiar to us, and we are posed no problem with regard to the nature of this solidarity that may be, according to the case, more or less close (to give some examples: religion, party, profession, etc.). If, among primitive men, this solidarity presents a more organic character, so individuals have there less real autonomy and less awareness of their own personality, it is not enough to stop us thinking that social solidarity is at heart essentially the same in those societies and in ours. Thus it seems that there is here no problem posed as in the case of participation through appurtenance or of the participation between the Naga and his leopard, of the bush soul, etc.

It is true that on looking more closely the social solidarity among the Australians is complicated by elements which do not appear in ours (and likewise in New Caledonia, among certain Bantu peoples, etc. . . .). It entails a participation with the earth (local totemic centres), with the mythical ancestors who shaped this earth and created those species, and so on. These are preoccupations that are not entirely familiar to us, and which it is not unprofitable to describe and analyse. I have even tried to 'understand' them—it is enough to remember all the attempts that have been made to try and make totemism (or the different sorts of totemism) intelligible, and the fact that the obscurities are not all dispersed and perhaps never will be entirely. Consequently it can no longer be said that there is no problem for us here: the basic participation remains for us as mysterious as the other forms cited earlier.

However, there remains a snag for me to avoid. In the present work there can be no question of giving a description or analysis of this participation with the supernatural, with the mythical beings, with the earth and its characteristics, etc., I have done it abundantly and perhaps overdone it in the series of volumes since the first, and in particular starting with Volume III. For no price am I willing to do it again and give the impression of repeating not only superfluously but in a poorer way what has been expounded previously. Therefore, it is necessary, if I make room (as it is probable) for this form of participation, essential, it might be said central to my subject, that I consider it under a new aspect, no longer simply a description of the facts but an effort to see of what this participation consists, and why the facts are as they appear to us; in short a study of the same type as that of participation through appurtenances, without harking back to the known facts. Difficult, but necessary.

January 1st, 1939.

Notebook X
January 1939

At the moment when I wanted to apply myself to the study of the Naga and his leopard type of participation, a passage from Elkin on the totem assistant caught my attention ('The secret life of the Australian Aborigines, *Oceania III*, p. 147,[1] more especially perhaps as Elkin himself does not emphasize it. 'The medicine man stands in a special relation to one natural species, usually an animal or reptile who acts as his assistant ... Such totems and 'familiars' are both within and without the individual. They are like a second self or spirit, and yet they are also externalized in the species, and may be exhibited in a tamed member of it.'

This second self, who is at the same time a 'familiar' or a totem rendering services to the individual and also a being exterior to him, in the form of a certain animal (usually a snake or a leopard) reminded me of the analogous beliefs with which I occupied myself at length in *The 'Soul' of the Primitive*. I have referred back to it and reread a good part of that book. The numerous cases of duality-unity that are given there, and the interpretation that is proposed, agree with my present thoughts, and have simultaneously the advantage of nourishing and stimulating them. In setting forth in *The 'Soul' of the Primitive* what are the individual totem of the North American Indians, the *nagual*, *nyarong*, etc., and also the wolfman of the Naga and the Malays, and again the *Kra*, *ntoro*, etc., of West Africa, I believe that I have shown that these beliefs directly involve a participation. I added that it is of the nature of these participations not to

---

[1] [Lévy-Bruhl has this reference wrong. The passage quoted appears to be a précis of pp. 113–14 of Elkin's article 'Studies in Australian totemism—The nature of Australian totemism', *Oceania*, Vol. IV, 1933–4. Translator's note]

be clearly understood and that one must not try to make transparent what, essentially, can only be opaque. Having reached this point, I judged it wise to go no further. The need to understand was satisfied only in a manner simultaneously very incomplete and final. I understood that there was no more to understand.

If, through the nature of things, I now find myself before the same insuperable obstacle, it is useless to return to the subject: I could only repeat what has been adequately demonstrated ten years ago. But it seems to me that I can now, if not resolve the problem declared unsolvable then, at least get a little closer to it, and not try to explain participations which cannot be explained, but, being no longer satisfied with having recognized this impossibility, try to explain a little better the reasons why.

For the universally attested cases of facts similar to the Australian totem assistant (who is at one and the same time within and without, second self, familiar, and snake or lizard): bush soul, lycanthropy, *nyarong*, etc., in brief for those obvious cases of duality-unity, let us first make a sincere effort to see the second term of this duality-unity with the same eyes as the primitive men who are convinced of its reality, which of course they do not state simply and unemotionally but the felt presence of which immediately awakes in them the characteristic and frequently confirmed emotion. It is not easy and the suppositions that we can make risk being dangerously unfounded: what means do we have of verifying them? One way seems open, however: to proceed with regard to these totem assistants, bush-souls, etc., as I have done, in this same work, with regard to appurtenances.

In brief: we have the habit of considering these only in their reality perceptible to the senses (kidney fat, soft and whitish substance, occupying a certain place, etc.). The Australians indeed have this representation as we do. But they also have another, which in *The 'Soul' of the Primitive* I already called mystical, and it is much more important in their eyes. The kidney fat felt as a mystical principle of life and lacking which the man invariably dies—(he recovers just like that if this principle, this fat, that has been stolen from him, is restored to him intact)—is no longer something purely material, only a soft and whitish substance, but it is also and above all a power, inseparable, it is true, from this substance but not confused with it, and by nature essentially mystical, that is to say belonging to the supernatural world, to the mythical world, and therefore outside the conditions of the physical world (conditions of time, space and secondary causes). An application of the formula 'every thing has an invisible being as well as a visible one'. Because it is invisible it can have an importance, a wealth of powers that one would never have thought of attributing to it if it were visible.

By virtue of this formula what we have said about appurtenances may equally well be said about the totem assistant, the bush soul, etc. . . . For us a snake or lizard is a certain animal, belonging to a certain class and species presenting a well defined form, granted such and such qualities and properties duly established by experience. We would never think of attributing to it other properties, imperceptible to our senses, nor think that it can have an existence distinct from that which we perceive, although linked to it (recall Elsdon Best). From this point of view it is completely unintelligible that something, existing outside the Australian's awareness and at a measurable distance from him, may be at the same moment *in* him, as a second self. However, the Australian is convinced of it: it is an undeniable fact. We, therefore, accept it without understanding it, without any hope of understanding it, and say that here is a participation which cannot be made intelligible.

Nevertheless, let us say that, like the kidney fat, this snake or lizard has an invisible existence and powers as well as a visible existence. It has been seen in Volumes V and VI that not only extraordinary animals that are not real animals but even real animals are not, in the eyes of primitive men, what they are in our eyes. They have an invisible existence, and even in their visible existence possess powers that inspire feelings that are definitely not felt in our civilization (recall the facts). From the point of view of the invisible existence in particular (and occasionally of the other) the primitive mentality does not place between animals and man (nor even between himself and plants and minerals) the insuperable distance that seems so obvious to us: the same *mana* circulates through all things.

Therefore there is nothing inconceivable or offensive for the primitive mentality in a snake or a lizard being the second self, the familiar of the medicine man. This second self is no more the

reptile that is known to us than the Australian's principle of life
is a lump of soft, whitish substance. In the case of the totem
assistant, of the bush soul, etc, the animal that is the second term
of the duality is not the simple animal that we perceive: it has a
double existence, and because this existence is mystical it escapes
the senses (the spiritual snakes of Fiji, the 'spiritual' bone in
pointing the bone, etc.). As a result of these considerations, the
participation between the Australian and his totem assistant,
between the African and his bush-soul (leopard, crocodile,
antelope) is clearly not explained nor even clarified. But it becomes less incredible, less disconcerting, less strange to our minds
so to speak. It no longer seems inconceivable to us that so many
'primitive men' happily accept this belief consistent with their
mental habits.

January 4th, 1939.

There is no need, with regard to the participations of the sort:
man-leopard, man-lion, man-crocodile, etc., to return to the fact
that in the eyes of the primitive mentality animals are not inferior
to man who often takes them for equals and sometimes for
superiors (in fact, the dead, who have gained rather than lost in
worth and mystical power, very often take the form of animals,
and this is surely one of the reasons for the attitude of the natives
with regard to certain species: tigers in Malaysia, lions in
southern Africa, crocodiles in west Africa, etc.). I have dealt with
the question, if not completely at least with the essential points,
in *La Mythologie Primitive*, pp. 54–70. I also tried to show how
beliefs relating to the duality-unity were linked to these beliefs
concerning animals. Therefore, all there is to do is to recall this
passage and refer to it.

What might rather lead to something new is the passage from
Elkin on the totem assistant quoted above (p. 1 of this notebook).
To begin with it makes it possible to define a characteristic form
of participation, clearly different from the participation between
the Naga and his leopard: participation between the totem without and the familiar within, the second self—which is equivalent
to an identity.

January 13th, 1939.

A QUESTION OF METHOD

I wonder if I have not been up against an impasse for some time and whether the task of going beyond what I have said up until now on the subject of participation is not impossible—or at least beyond my abilities. I have reviewed with care the facts about participation—in particular duality-unity—that are collected in large number in *The 'Soul' of the Primitive* and *La Mythologie Primitive*: I do not see how I could at the moment throw more light on them or extend their interpretation. Even Elkin's very explicit text relating to the totem assistant, quoted above, puts the difficulty into relief rather than suggesting a solution. And I fear that other analogous facts that it would doubtless not be difficult to add to those that I have already assembled do not serve to lead further.

It is natural that these findings that assert themselves, and to which there is no objection, give rise to a reappraisal. The impasse (if it is real and final) leads to a closer examination of the terms in which the question is posed, and whether other terms would not have been preferable, that is to say, whether by taking another, apparently less direct way, I would not have had more chance, if not of reaching the goal at least of getting closer to it.

To come to grips with a deeper study of what participation is, while being convinced that to make it intelligible is to misrepresent it and that one must not seek to clarify this obscure mental reality or make its opacity transparent, is worse than a paradox, it is to claim to make a movement for which one is paralysed in advance and knows it. A hopeless enterprise and thus foolish. Furthermore, if, for once in a while, the efforts had the appearance of success, the result would be without objective value, and equivalent to the success of a skilful conjuring trick.

Therefore to drop the idea, not of going a little further than the preceding works, but of a frontal attack clearly condemned in advance to failure, that is to say to examine whether, by another way, it would be possible to turn the obstacle that appears insurmountable.

January 17th, 1939.

N

MEANING OF 'IS NOT CONCEPTUAL'

Of ways other than that by which I have failed, I perceive only
two at the moment. I have already thought about them more
than once, but without ever making a serious effort to see whether
they would lead me nearer the goal.

The first thing would be to try to analyse as deeply as possible
the affective element that is essential to participation. So far I
have only mentioned it, in saying that participation is felt rather
than thought. Each time I described it I indicated that by its
nature it is recalcitrant to analysis, and therefore we cannot make
use of the method that customarily renders facts intelligible to us,
at least up to a certain point. All facts, of course, do not present
the same type of complexity and do not allow themselves likewise
to be resolved into elements that are easy to grasp and isolate by
the means that we have at our disposal and that are sometimes
extremely inadequate.

In the past the exploration of what is affective has never led
very far; it has always been halted quickly enough by an
obscurity on which the light of understanding has not spread
much illumination. However, this is not a decisive reason for not
trying this way: the worst that can happen is that I find it as
unproductive as the preceding way. In any case, through this
attempt I will perhaps find some help with ideas that relate to
the affective category of the supernatural on one side, and to the
mystical experience on the other. I have already recalled the
words of Leenhardt when he came to talk after he had read
Primitives and the Supernatural: 'The affective category of the
supernatural is participation, isn't it?' The feeling, so right and
so profound, that he has of the primitive mentality had shown
him the closest affinity between participation and the perception
of the supernatural, and even more than an affinity, undoubtedly
two aspects of a single mental reality. Without doubt there is an
advantage for me to examine as closely as possible this affinity, or
better said, this community of nature between the feeling of a
participation and the feeling of the supernatural. Whether what
I will be able to determine applies to all cases of participation, or
only to certain of them, this investigation will not be without
result perhaps.

To be honest, it has been started already, although in an indirect way, since my objective was different in the researches that I made concerning the mystical experience, and that have confirmed me in the idea that it is indeed in reality an experience but an experience that has at the same time its own characteristics, of which the most essential is the feeling of contact with the world of invisible beings, of the supernatural: a contact that is always accompanied by an emotion which primitive men do not mistake. Consequently the constant affective feature characterizing this experience is the feeling of a contact with the supernatural. Therefore to speak of mystical experience is *ipso facto* to speak of the affective category of the supernatural; and, according to Leenhardt's idea, of participation at the same time.—Again, there would therefore be an advantage for me to reconsider the mystical experience from the point of view of the question that I am now asking myself and that did not concern me when I wrote the fifth volume: not 'what does the feeling of participation consist of', terms in which I no longer wish to ask the question; but 'how feeling of contact with the supernatural (mystical experience), emotion *sui generis* that is inseparable from it (affective category of the supernatural) and participation are intrinsically more than intimately linked'.

January 17th, 1938.

In appearance the other route is more round about. It starts from an observation that is already to be found in *How Natives Think* and that recurs often enough in the subsequent works: to realize that among primitive men thought is not conceptual. But since I expressed it for the first time this observation has taken on a new, deeper and richer sense. To begin with it emphasized a characteristic that distinguishes, particularly from the logical point of view, the primitive mentality from ours in showing that very often they have names, sometimes very numerous, for the varieties and sub-varieties of a plant species and do not have a term for the species itself; for the sweeps and bends of a river, each designated by a name, and none for the river, etc. . . . I used to associate this tendency with their way of abstracting and generalizing. Thus I kept to the territory common to psychology and logic in considerations concerning discursive thought.

Little by little the facts have led me to understand that it is not
so simple as it had first seemed to me. The formula: their thought
is not conceptual is not tenable. Just like us, they have the power
to form concepts and the proof of this is to be found in their
languages, which sometimes, to our surprise, have abstract terms
comparable with ours and even corresponding exactly (Bantu).

Accordingly it is right to modify the formula thus: their
thought is not conceptual in the same way as ours is, they do not
make the same use of their power to form concepts as we do. And
if, as is natural, we seek the cause for this difference, we then see
that the formula has the fault of presupposing the postulates of
traditional western psychology and logic, and that we are wrong
in seeking to characterize primitive men's 'thought', implying by
that the function of thought (διάνοια). I have had occasion to
insist on their aversion to the most simple operations of 'discursive thought' and it is this aversion to a sort of unaccustomed
mental activity that I wanted to express in saying that their
thought is not conceptual—I now see that it is an inaccurate, and
even misleading formula.

January 19th, 1939.

If we thus renounce putting the problem in traditional and too
inadequate terms, what terms can we use? By what expressions
will we replace 'their thought is not conceptual'?—In reply to
this question it is necessary to introduce the results obtained since
The 'Soul' of the Primitive and particularly those from the last
three volumes: roughly, that it is not a matter of thought properly
so called but of complexes where the representational elements
are inseparable from the emotional elements—that primitive
men's experience comprises what I have called mystical experience besides what it has in common with our experience—that
those minds are thus oriented differently from ours—that their
belief in myths familiarizes them with the representation of a
world where fluidity dominates—that, as a result, they do not
have our idea of what is physically impossible by virtue of the
regularity of the laws of nature and the fixity of specific forms.

All these results, essential characteristics of the primitive mentality, allow an understanding of its world view (*Weltanschauung*):
it is something much wider and vaster than the more specific and

precise character that I had believed that I had grasped and expressed through the formula 'their thought is not conceptual'. In fact, this whole world view (*Weltanschauung*) of which I have just recalled the principal traits involves the affective category of the supernatural, and as a result, if Leenhardt's words are accepted, it is closely linked to participation. Thus we are brought back to our problem, which we had seemed to be leaving behind, and perhaps we can define with some precision the direction in which the 'second way' ought to lead us, or, more accurately, in which direction it may allow us to advance. This is not yet established; on the contrary it is still to be found: to find how the formula whose inexactness we see ought to be changed in order to be included in the collection of results obtained in the successive volumes (above all in Volumes V and VI): or, in other words, to find the middle terms that assure the link between, on one side, what we expressed badly through 'their thought is not conceptual like ours'—and, on the other side, the primitive mentality's world view (*Weltanschauung*); to show that one is attached to the other, and to indicate as far as possible how the passage, the connection, is made. If I managed to elucidate this—in any case I can try at the risk of not succeeding—this 'second way' would have had its usefulness.

January 20th, 1939.

THE FUNCTIONS OF CONCEPTS

To begin with let us try this 'second way'. The starting point is the attempt to disengage what might be right in the admittedly inadequate formula 'their thought is not conceptual like ours' (*How Natives Think*). To abandon the idea that they do not form concepts like us; their languages are enough to make this be rejected.

But what I do not abandon and what seems well proved by the facts (Cherokee, Australian, etc.) is that concepts have not become for them, as they have for us, the precision instruments of a discursive thought, a logical material invaluable for recording established knowledge and for use in acquiring new knowledge: one of the most marked differences between them and us is just their aversion to more or less abstract reasoning.

Accordingly the first step in our research ought to be: what is the reason for this difference? It is not to be found in the concepts themselves, although it may be true that for the most part they possess fewer of the very general and abstract concepts than we do, and they stay closer to the concrete reality. The reason lies deeper and is connected with the essential characteristics of the primitive mentality. These prevent it from making the logical use of concepts that seems so easy and almost natural to us. In effect, in the primitive mentality the mystical experience is placed on the same footing as the other; it has at least as much, if not more authority and value than the other, and in the case of conflict it is most often it that prevails: it forms part of the human experience, taken in its totality, as does the other.

The direct consequence is that the concepts of things and natural objects cannot fill the same functions for them as for us. At any moment a mystical experience can contradict the assertion implied in the concept (Hume made it clearly seen that the idea always implies a judgement). Example: wild boars come to ravage the manioc plantations (Gabon). But are they really wild boars? May it not rather be the irate dead who have disguised themselves thus (Miss. evangelical. 1938)? Likewise in Indonesia, the birds that pilfer the crops, and everywhere animals whose looks seem rather unusual, plants that deviate from the normal, in brief everything that is *mease* (and that appears unexpectedly on endless occasions). When it is not a matter of 'genuine' animals or plants, then the name is no longer legitimately applied to them, nor is the concept; then it is necessary to guard against concluding anything about them that derives from the ordinary concept. The 'genuine' jaguar can be hunted and killed; but the *kanaima* jaguar, despite its similar external appearance, at least with regard to shape, to that of other jaguars, is impossible to do away with and it is excessively dangerous to have dealings with it. It is not an animal, it is a witch, a maleficent power that has judged it expedient to take momentarily this form. The concept here is of no use.

If therefore the concepts that the primitive mentality is in principle capable of forming and that it often forms, as does our mentality, do not render it the same services and do not provide the same logical material that they do for our mentality, the reason is now evident: it resides in the mystical orientation of the primitive mentality, that is to say in the objective value that they recognize in the mystical experience (dreams, etc.) and in the feeling of the relations between the natural and the supernatural that is completely different among primitive men from among us. As has been seen in Volumes V and VI, the decisive point is the following: for us, the natural phenomena are ruled by virtually indispensable laws, that is to say that, in our usual experience, they never contradict themselves; and equally the specific forms of the objects in nature (animal, vegetable or mineral) are also fixed, in practice, in our actual experience, whatever may have been their evolution in the past, or what it might be in the future. This necessity, this fixity are inscribed, incorporated in our concepts which embody them, so to speak. This allows us to operate logically on these concepts, and to consider the result of these operations as valid for the things and objects in nature—whence the possibility of science and the success of its application.

But in the minds of primitive men neither this necessity of laws nor this fixity of forms is inseparable from the concepts of things and objects. Doubtless they form concepts as well, and incorporate them in languages as well. But, at the same time, by virtue of their traditional mental orientation and of their confidence in the mystical experience, they do not accept that there is anything physically impossible, that is to say that the supernatural powers may at any moment intervene in, interrupt or modify the normal course of things. The concepts are there in vain: they no longer involve the indispensability of the order of nature and the fixity of forms. Therefore primitive men cannot make the same use of them as we do; it is even impossible for them to represent this usage. For them it fits into that collection of incomprehensible (and surely magical) practices that they call 'way of the white men".

Here is the core of the truth that was enclosed in the inadequate formula and that explains why this formula found a place in *How Natives Think*. It remains to be known whether this correction can be of some help to us in penetrating a little further into the primitive mentality's peculiar form.

January 22nd, 1939.

Take care to distinguish the logical usage of concepts in abstract reasoning, of which we have just been speaking, and

their purely practical use in daily life. The primitive mentality
has no training in the first; education does not prepare it as oral
tradition and above all schooling does among us (all teaching
proceeds in a more or less abstract fashion, particularly in France,
and calculus and arithmetic give everyone the knowledge of
handling ideally abstract concepts, so to speak).—There is nothing like this among primitive men whose aversion to even the
simplest problems is characteristic (Junod). But they have, just
like us, the second, purely practical use of concepts, which comes
back to saying that from this point of view their languages render
the same services as ours do; they have no need of grammar,
analyses or reflection of any sort for the employment that they
make, like us, of names, verbs, pronouns, etc.; from this point of
view the abstraction involved in language (formation of concepts)
occurs with the spontaneity that characterizes the functions of the
organism.

January 23rd, 1939.

THE TWO USES OF CONCEPTS

If I return to the formula from *How Natives Think*: 'their
thought is not conceptual like ours', just as I should have sought
to be adequately precise concerning the formation and use of
concepts considered both among them and us, so also I should
grasp more closely what sense to give to the word thought. Otherwise it is not univocal. Their thought, *qua* thought, differs from
ours, as their concepts *qua* concepts—although it may be true
that in principle their mind forms concepts as ours does, and
thinks like ours. Therefore it is necessary to attempt an analysis
of the facts that permits us to grasp, under the identity of the
function of thought, the differences of this function's product,
and, if possible, their causes.

Perhaps we might in approaching 'thought' follow the same
route as we did in approaching 'concepts', since in this last
research it led to a result. We found that the difference occurred
not in the concepts themselves but in the use that was made of
them.

We have even been led to distinguish two sorts of uses of concepts: one that is common both to the primitive mentality and

ours, and that consists essentially in the concepts' application to daily needs, to the solution of problems of behaviour that everyday life continually presents, the endless contact with natural phenomena, the objects and things, animals, other members of the family, social group, etc. . . . This usage is expressed, reflected and conveyed faithfully in the language: this only has to be observed in the employment that primitive men, like us, make of names and verbs, etc. . . .—Another use of concepts consists in making them the singularly powerful instrument, made easy by practice, of reasoning and thought (διάνοια): to form a hierarchy of firm but plastic concepts that makes classification possible, the different degrees of abstraction, and lastly a whole series of intellectual operations thanks to which mental life and, *pari passu*, the knowledge of nature make progress that, in turn, provides new possibilities. Now this use of concepts is not familiar to the primitive mentality; it instinctively avoids it so to speak and often when one tries to accustom it there to, it turns aside from it, at least to begin with (cf. *La Mythologie Primitive*).

Likewise, we say, the minds of 'primitive men' have the same capacity to think as we do, and when indeed they think they think like us: they are men like us. Where the difference appears is in the use made by them and by us of this capacity to think. Here again, there are grounds, it seems, for distinguishing two sorts of use. One that is common to them and us and that consists, as in the case of concepts, in the application of thought to the solution of questions of behaviour that daily life presents at every moment when the solution is not furnished immediately or imposed by tradition, as it often is (education, imitation of the preceding generation, precepts learned from the ancestors, etc.). This use of thought reveals a so to speak vital function of the intelligence, one as useful in the defence of the individual as the purely physiological functions: Schopenhauer, after the eighteenth-century French philosophers, has demonstrated this well. This first use of thought is inseparable from the first use of concepts which has been spoken of earlier. Like the use of language it does not require reflection: it occurs in a spontaneous fashion, and, like the other vital functions, when the needs of life demand to be satisfied—with this reservation, however, that this 'thinking' function, like language, is only found in the human species.

For a stronger reason, the other use of the capacity of thought will be an exclusive privilege of man; the use that is no longer simply vital, instinctive, and so to speak physiological—but reflective and bearing on objects that are not brought and imposed on him by the needs of life, but on the contrary are, to a greater or lesser extent, the products of his own activity: now it is in this peculiarly human use of thought that the difference between the primitive mentality and ours is manifested with clarity. Until now I have characterized it by saying that this mentality is mystically oriented, whence it results that it has some habits and tendencies different from ours. Now, following *La Mythologie Primitive* and *L'Expérience Mystique et les Symboles chez les Primitifs* I can try to be more precise.

Now in so far as their mental habits contrast with ours what first is striking about them is the little attention that they give to even the most simple logical operations for which the primitive mentality seems to have at least an indifference if not an aversion. In other words, it makes no use of that unparalleled instrument the concepts. This is what we have stated earlier. But we can now go a step further: we cannot only state this well established fact, but give an explanation for it. It is to be found in the difference between primitive men's experience and our own: the former is simultaneously positive and mystical in an inextricable way, ours normally excludes the mystical facts that the other accepts without difficulty as being as valuable as those of verifiable and checkable experience. From this difference known consequences flow: the fluidity of the natural world even, where there can be neither necessary laws nor fixed types since the invisible forces may at any moment intervene in, interrupt or modify the regular course of phenomena: whence the tendency to allow that nothing is physically impossible, etc. . . .

But the concepts are precisely the reservoirs where the results of the non-mystical experience are collected, deposited and organized. Through them is expressed the regularity of the phenomena, the order of nature, that is to say the necessity of laws and the permanence of forms: we have seen that in daily behaviour the primitive mentality makes use of these concepts as we do. But because it is mystically oriented, that is to say in so far as it grants the mystical experience a value at least equal to that of the other experience, it has nothing to make of these concepts whose essential characteristics it denies by its very practice. Thus we not only see that 'this thought is not conceptual like ours' but we see why. It could not be otherwise without renouncing its mystical orientation and without ceasing to endow the mystical experience with the objectivity and validity that makes it more precious and sacred (if not more objective) than the experience that is common to us and them. Therefore it is evident that the primitive mentality cannot have the same habits and tendencies as ours, which brings us back to saying that it is not conceptual, while discerning for what reasons it could not be.

Thus, by the same right, we can say either that, mystically oriented, that is to say penetrated by the value of the mystical experience, the thought of 'primitive men' does not proceed by logical operations on the concepts and does not incorporate the products of its activity in concepts involving an intelligible order, as we do,—or else that the concepts, indispensable in daily behaviour and so valuable for the development of positive experience, have nothing to attract a thought that is oriented mystically and that is at least as preoccupied by the facts of the mystical experience as those of the other (as is seen by the place that, for example, dreams hold in the life of primitive men, and especially the dead whose feelings, warning and reactions are at least as important to them as those of the living). It now remains to be seen what this thought that is not conceptual is.

January 30th, 1939.

Notebook XI
February 1939

I. Non-conceptual *thought*. In what sense exactly to take the word to think?—To distinguish the point of view of action and of thought more or less conscious of itself and reflective. The latter is not developed in logical operations. Of what then does it consist?

II. Above all else, to take account of the importance and the characteristics of the mystical experience and to consider separately the different cases.

    1. Where the mystical experience and the other are inextricably intertwined, thought can no longer be considered in isolation. The emotional elements gain the upper hand, without eliminating the representational elements (examples: shark, etc.). In place of a backcloth of ordered and intelligible nature, the supernatural and fluidity. To what extent can this complex be called experience or belief? Part of the tradition.

    2. Mystical experience properly so called, without actual mixture with the other experience (presence of words, dreams). Importance of the emotional element: not of thought *stricto sensu*—then the effort of interpretation (the data are signs). Transition to 2: myth, kin of the dream.

III. This non-conceptual thought, free of the conditions of space and time, and consequently of causality as we understand it: but based on direct causality (efficient power in itself)—free also of numeration—(consubstantiality of what appears distinct: for example duality-unity, bi- and multi-presence).

IV. To show the close relationship of this 'thought'. 1. with the idea: everything has an invisible existence as well as a visible one. 2. with participation, and even participation as *inherent* in this thought.

    In this way, participation is not 'explained'—it cannot be and

179

ought not to be, it has no need of legitimation; but one sees its
necessary place in the human mind—and as a result its role in
religion, in metaphysics, in art and even in the conception of the
whole of nature.

February 2nd, 1939.

NON-CONCEPTUAL THOUGHT AND MYSTICAL EXPERIENCE

One of the reasons, and perhaps the principal one, that ensures
that primitive men's thought is not conceptual results from the
fact that their experience, wider than ours, is often mystical, and,
as such, is unaware of the ordered regularity of the sequences of
phenomena like the fixity of forms; it moves in a mythical world
of which the most striking characteristic is fluidity. Thus is explained that this thought, although capable of forming concepts,
makes no great use of them (outside daily practical life) and does
not engage in the logical operations that the concepts make
available, with the help of abstraction, classification, etc. . . .
I have examined this point in Notebook X.

It remains to see whether, in this formula, the word 'thought'
is univocal, whether indeed it has the same sense, the same range,
the same implications, when it is a question of primitive men
and when it concerns us. If one reflects on the characteristics by
which the mystical experience contrasts with the other, one is
tempted to give a negative answer. In short, ordinary experience
involves confidence in an intelligible order that constitutes a
'nature', undoubtedly extremely complicated, but of which the
advances through experience (and later, through science) allow
us to discover slowly the laws, independently of the fact that the
more our knowledge is enriched the more numerous and complex
the problems grow: which, doubtless, makes us less presumptuous
and more aware of the enormity of the task, but does not dis-
courage us. Indeed to the contrary, the little that we have learned,
sound although always submitted to revision when some new
points of view are revealed, is a guarantee to us at one and the
same time of the order of nature and of the validity of the thought
that scrutinizes and analyses it.

In other words, nature does not admit of miracles (things
happen in nature because their causes are given in it) nor of

mysteries in the full sense of the word, of mysteries other than temporary ones, that is to say mysteries until the advances of experience and science have made us capable of resolving them. And the fact that the number of unresolved mysteries increases rather than diminishes does not shake the human mind's faith in itself. Unresolved, perhaps in fact without solution for an unlimited time, the mysteries of nature are none the less resolvable in principle. The inadequacy of the means that thought has at its disposal in the presence of one of these mysteries does not weaken its courage, nor slow its efforts. In its own eyes, its value remains intact, and its discoveries, that are so little in comparison with the complexity of things, confirms it in the feeling that it renders the world more and more intelligible.

Completely different is the world into which the mystical experience introduces us. Properly speaking, it does not introduce us to it: it simply reveals to us its existence, it make us feel its presence, but its data, although often making the deepest impression, do not lend themselves to minute observation, to experimentation, to analysis. This world is invisible, and doubtless in essence mysterious: there is no question of dissipating this mystery through methodical effort of research pursued by successive generations of scientists. This is not a domain open to knowledge, and one of which the boundaries retreat to the measure and extent that knowledge advances. It is before all a cause of the emotions which penetrate to the very depth of the imagination and heart, fear, hope, respect, submission, and later confidence, love—in short, the whole emotional gamut that forms part of the religious experience.

Thus man finds himself here in contact, not with a natural but with a supernatural world. His experience is not for him a means of getting to know it, but a warning of what he can fear or hope from it; he will try to question it, to divine the impending action of the supernatural forces, to interpret the frequently enigmatic and ambiguous signs by which this action is announced or revealed. As a result this supernatural world has a completely different character from the natural one: the structure remains blurred and vague, and there is little effort to make it more precise and definite. How do they represent it? Naturally we do not have direct evidence on that; primitive men do not ask themselves questions of this sort, and have never thought about the answer to give. But we can give ourselves an idea of what they think about it from their myths and from the ceremonies where they put myths into action. This is why it is not too risky to show what the supernatural is for them from the mythical world that is familiar to them. And the examination of this mythical world will allow us to disengage what is peculiar to the 'thought' that is preoccupied by it, in so far as it is distinguished from the 'thought' that operates on nature by the means of concepts.

This thought, which is necessarily conditioned by the organization common to all human minds, thus acts in conformity with the laws of that organization. For example, in the presence of an experience of a phenomenon or an accident, it immediately seeks the cause, as we do. But it does not proceed as we do in this search. In *La Mythologie Primitive* I have always tried to show where it seeks the cause. It does not attribute great importance to the nexus of secondary causes or the chain of phenomena in regular series where the antecedents are followed by the consequences. It is not unaware of these sequences, and as required it turns them to its advantage. But for it, here are only instruments mostly of occasional causes at the service of the true cause which is somewhere else, that is to say in the world of forces we call supernatural, and which have intervened in the world of natural phenomena in order to produce there (in the strong sense of the word), in order to determine there the effect which properly reveals its intervention.

Causality thus understood or felt cannot be 'thought' in the same way as our causal nexus. It is immediately seen—not by way of logical or dialectical consequence, but in the facts themselves, and in the language held by primitive men—that the efficient action of the cause is independent of the conditions of time and space. This is a property that originates in what belongs to the supernatural world. It works as well at a distance as close to (bewitching in Paris of someone in Rome); it acts instantaneously or is delayed as it likes, whatever happens in the interval, etc. . . .

February 3rd, 1939.

MYSTICAL EXPERIENCE AND TWO CAUSALITIES

In the explanation that precedes is always implied the distinction
(much less important for us than for primitive men) between the
facts, normal things and phenomena, and those things that make
their impression through their abnormal character. Everything
that is familiar, customary, and conforms with previous experience goes without comment and is accepted without particular
emotion (except of course the cases whereby a danger is thus
announced, but is a known danger, catalogued, so to speak, and
which it is known how to parry or escape from). The more or less
complicated reaction then occurs among them as among us, that
is to say by a series of means or processes in which there is taken
into fullest account the causal connections (in our sense) that
bring about or turn away such a foreseen result. This use of the
regular sequences of phenomena, which involves causality as we
understand it, is evident in their techniques, that are sometimes so
ingenious and clever, traps for animals, in particular for fish,
agriculture, gardens, basketry, pottery, etc.: and it is remarkable
that the magical operations that are considered as no less indispensable for success than the techniques properly so called, do
not prevent the 'primitive man' from giving all his attention to
the positive technique, and from neglecting none of the 'ante-
cedent' actions that could bring about the expected consequence
or prevent it from occurring.

But when it is a matter of something extraordinary or abnormal, that departs from the usual, the attitude changes abruptly.
In so far as it is a matter of normal phenomena and things, the
primitive mentality takes them as they are and does not make
them an object of reflection. The normal causal connections do
not surprise it at all, and it simply establishes and utilizes these
connections between phenomena (for example, in techniques)
with care when it needs it, but also without any emotion. At the
appearance of something abnormal, on the contrary, there occurs
immediately an emotion, *sui generis* and generally violent. Because it is for the primitive mentality the revelation—beyond
doubt—of the presence and the action of an invisible power, that
is going to bring misfortune (for example, the definition of *measa*,
of which Kruyt cites innumerable cases). And as the primitive

o

mentality, particularly under the onset of an emotion, does not distinguish between sign and cause, the *malum augurium* proves by its presence alone the action of a cause belonging to the supernatural world. Thus if in a house where a chicken crows like a cock—which is *measa*—someone falls ill, a child dies, the harvest is ravaged by wild boars or rats, etc., what so happens is no longer explained by the simple chain of phenomena, even if this chain habitually takes place. The cause is in the action of the supernatural force, and only in it. (Recall here some striking examples: the spear blow in Papua—the men killed by the thunderbolt in French Equatorial Africa, etc.).

Now, whereas for normal phenomena the primitive mentality behaves as if it realized that things only happen if their antecedents occur, even if it does not formulate the law of causality that it establishes, and even takes the application in advance for certain—as soon as it is a matter of something unusual or abnormal, of an anomaly, of an accident or a misfortune, it suddenly becomes indifferent to this law, and the causal nexus has no more than a secondary importance which leaves it indifferent. All its often impassioned attention centres on the presumed real cause, which belongs to the world of supernatural forces, and the question how seems to lose all interest. It is that in such cases there is no question of a secondary cause, itself caused by one or many antecedents forming part of an irreversible series of links—but rather indeed of a primary cause, that is to say a cause has in itself the power to engender or realize its effect. This is not the omnipotent—the primitive mentality does not rise to this abstract concept—but has the same value: it is a power of the same order that realizes its effect equally well by any means of its choice (examples, French West Africa, New Guinea, etc.) or even, at need, by entirely dispensing with means (with a chain of secondary causes).

Direct consequences: 1. At the same time this action is independent of the conditions of place and time, which are undoubtedly indispensable when it is a matter of secondary causes (nexus, series of phenomena occurring *hic at nunc*). A primary cause is enough for the action, and it is futile wanting to represent how it happens. 2. The nature where such causes operate necessarily retains the fluidity of the mythical world.

February 4th, 1939.

This indifference to the conditions of place and time, and as a result to the natural causality which is inseparable from them, that characterizes the 'thought' of primitive men as soon as they are under the influence of the mystical experience, is found, as is known, with complete evidence, in the perception of dreams, a mystical experience of the first order, and which, in their eyes, has at least as much validity and significance as the participations experienced in the waking state. In dreams, at least in those in which the primitive mentality recognizes the normal value, the actions and things do not absolutely depend on conditions of place and time, nor on causal nexuses (examples: journey to the land of the dead, transformation of objects, etc.). The man who has dreamt is perfectly aware of this character of the experiences given in the dream, but he does not conclude from it that these experiences are illusory. What is so given is real. The primitive man is not concerned to know *how* this reality accords with what *we* consider to be the necessary conditions of reality. The reality is sufficient in itself since it is imposed. This is the case with all mystical experience. Recall the affinity between dreams and myth.

February 7th, 1939.

SOCIAL DEFENCE AGAINST CONTAGION

An observation recorded among the Kipsigis allows a better understanding of facts reported over a long time from the most different civilizations. It is a matter of the contagious impurity of female blood under certain circumstances (menstruation, child-birth, etc.). After giving birth the Kipsigis woman must absolutely not touch anything, nor take anything in her hands, not even what she eats or drinks. If she touches milk the cows of the village will become sterile, if she touches the corn porridge the field will dry up. If, during the following months, she touches some objects without washing her hands every object of the same type will be *ipso facto* soiled and lost, unusable.

Now 1. this prohibition, for the woman temporarily impure, from touching food and drink with her own hands, has been observed many times (Indians of the Pacific North-West Coast, of North America, Maoris, etc.). The Kipsigis case furnishes us with an explanation of it. The taboo does not have as its object the protection of the young girl who comes to puberty. It is a measure of social defence. If the young girl touched her food or drink, all the similar food and drink of the group would be rendered impure at the same instance and would become a public danger. It is known that mourning taboos very closely resemble those taboos that are imposed on the young girl at the time of her first menstruation and at childbirth (at least in certain societies). It is because the impurity arising from contact with the dead man or from a close relationship with him (husband and wife, parents and children) is inevitably diffused through the other members of the group if they are not separated from the bearers of the impurity. This diffusion objectively expresses for the members of the group the same feeling of fear as the taboo that forbids the young girl or the new mother from touching food and drink with her hands. It might even be asked whether the pollution produced through the contact of the woman's hand with her food and drink does not prefigure, for the primitive mentality, the soiling that will result for other food, and whether by prefiguring it does not cause it.

February 7th, 1939.

INDIFFERENCE TO THE DISTINCTION BETWEEN ONE AND MANY

Where do these so widely spread beliefs come from, and how does the primitive mentality represent to itself the idea that if the woman in labour touches an object with her hands, all similar objects are soiled *ipso facto* like it?—The material for the answer to these questions is to be found, at least for the main part, in *Primitives and the Supernatural.* There it is shown that neither dirt nor contagion has for primitive men the same positive sense that they have for us. A pollution is a bewitchment, that is to say, it is not possible to speak of it without being transported in thought into the world of mystical experience, of supernatural forces; that is amply proved in the study of witchcraft which occupies a long chapter in that same work. But, from the moment it is a matter of an action of this sort, from the moment the contagion of the dirt is a *mystical* infection, we are in the region where no one is concerned with knowing how the event occurs.

The sequence of phenomena does not count (so little does it that despite the distance the contagion is often thought as direct). The only thing that matters, besides the infection itself, is its true cause which it is important to combat and neutralize as quickly as possible by removing from it the means of operation; whence the numerous taboos relating to menstrual blood, and their singular resemblance to mourning taboos. The avoidance of defilement, that is to say witchcraft. If it has occurred, free oneself from it immediately.

As to the fact that all objects similar to that which the impure woman has touched are *ipso facto* defiled like it, the primitive mentality states it and does not feel the need to explain it, no more than it does the sickness of the cow whose milk this woman has drunk. It does not think of asking itself how the supernatural power proceeds: it 'focuses' simply on its inevitable results. But we can note that, in the region of mystical action whither we find ourselves transported, just as this action is transcendental with regard to the conditions of time and place, and indifferent to the nexuses of natural causality—likewise it is indifferent to the distinction between one and many: this is what I have called the diffusion of pollution. Mystical diffusion, like pollution itself, and to the degree it is represented, is transcendant.

February 7th, 1939.

ATTEMPT AT EXPLANATION

What hampers me and what prevents me from reaching if not a complete elucidation (that is evidently impossible) at least a relatively satisfactory one is that I am obeying two tendencies that are not simply distinct but opposed, and I am thus being pulled in two diverging directions.

On one side, I make use of the distinction between the mystical experience and the other experience, which allows me to explain certain facts: for example that the primitive mentality, in daily practice and in its techniques, conforms to the causal nexus between phenomena arrived at by observation that is sometimes careful and minute; but that this same mentality no longer pays much attention to this nexus nor to the conditions of time and place as soon as it is in the presence of a supernatural force whose action is revealed by an accident, a misfortune, a sickness, a death, something unaccustomed or abnormal, or as soon as it itself makes appeal to forces of this type (white and black magic, charms necessary for the success of every enterprise, etc.).

But at the same time I see more and more clearly that the distinction between the two sorts of experience (although well founded on the feeling that primitive men very obviously have characteristics peculiar to the mystical experience) cannot be rigorously maintained, and that there is for the primitive mentality (I do not say for us who study it) only a single experience, sometimes mixed, sometimes almost entirely mystical, sometimes almost entirely non-mystical, but undoubtedly never exclusively one or the other.

This is what I indicated, although in an imperfect way, in *How Natives Think* when I insisted on the mystical character of the primitive mentality taken *in globo* (I did not then distinguish between the mystical experience and the other experience) when I used to say that primitive men do not perceive anything as we do; I should rather have said: do not perceive anything *entirely* as we do. Today perhaps I can get a little closer to an exact expression of the facts if I say that the mystical orientation of this mentality makes itself felt more or less strongly or weakly, even when their experience and their ways of acting seem completely parallel to ours; continually variable nuances, difficult to determine and still more to express.

February 9th, 1939.

The recourse to fact, the examination of a concrete example will doubtless be preferable to an abstract analysis. An animal which the primitive man is accustomed to hunt or to flee from appears before his eyes. In what way does the perception that he has differ from the one we have, in what way, on this occasion, does he think differently from us? It seems that if we grasp exactly what happens in his mind, we would find that the associations of ideas and feelings (accompanied by motor reactions) that follow are not entirely the same as in our minds, which is not at all surprising given the difference in surroundings, education, customs, beliefs, but nevertheless the perception is essentially similar and the concept is also to the extent that it simply corresponds with the name that designates the animal.

However, one cannot stop there, on pain of remaining very superficial. We know that in such an encounter the primitive man is prepared to wonder, at the slightest opportunity, whether he is dealing with a genuine animal or with a thing which is not an animal but which has taken on the appearance of one. Probably in order to hurt him. There is more. Even if the animal appears to him to be genuine and ordinary, he does not have (all reflection aside) an idea of it similar to ours. Our idea, even among ignorant and uncultured people, is zoological: it classifies the animal in its place among the living things which are more or less close to it: they simply think: it is a hare, it is a crocodile, it is a snake, etc. . . . But for the primitive man, each animal is distinguished from the others, not by its morphological and anatomical features, etc., but by the powers of which it disposes: in this way an animal that is entirely inoffensive in our eyes can be dangerous in theirs. Mystical elements enter into the idea they have of it, and the simple encounter with the animal can determine in the primitive man an emotion of which we have no suspicion. Thus we must not judge what happens then in his mind by our own experience in a similar case, nor take as agreed that he 'thinks' then as we do. What we have just said shows that this would be wrong.

Another, no less important difference, also already indicated in *How Natives Think*, but without my having sufficiently insisted on it there (pp. 100–2): 'What above all interests this mentality in the animal . . . is the spirit of which it is the manifestation . . . Invisible and intangible, this spirit is at one and the same time in all of them and in each of them . . . It was believed that the birds killed at the same annual feast in a large number of widely separated villages were all one and the same bird.'

In other words, which I use in preference today, we here establish a fact of the same order as the indifference to the conditions of time and place when it is a matter of facts, and that the primitive man, above all attentive to the mystical elements of an experience, ascribes the cause to a supernatural force, and neglects the nexus of secondary causes which then play a subordinate and completely unnecessary role, and in certain cases do not even play that, the supernatural cause having the power to produce by itself and alone the result. Equally, if it is no longer a question of events but of living things, when the primitive man has his attention fixed on their mystical elements and on their powers, the distinction between the individual animals, among themselves and also of the mystical essence that is common to them is neglected: for each one only possesses these powers thanks to this invisible essence of which they are the visible realization in the given experience; at one and the same time perishable and indestructible. Perishable since men kill and eat them; at the same time indestructible because the essence that makes them what they are is totally unreachable, and because in certain conditions the slaughtered animals are reborn (Rasmussen, Indian story in *La Mythologie Primitive*) just as dead humans are sometimes reincarnated and return to life.

Leenhardt has well shown that primitive men have the idea of death only to the extent that they have the idea of individuality, and the converse. To the degree that the individual does not conceive of his existence as detachable from that of the group, no more does he conceive that he can cease to exist when he ceases to live: he simply changes residence. Now what is true of man is no less true of animals. No more do they, on dying, cease to exist. Hence, in so many societies, the honours rendered to slain animals, particularly to those of which the mystical powers are considerable (bears, tigers, leopards, elephants, eagles, etc.); hence the precautions taken to protect the animal killer, like the murderer; hence, again, the very widespread belief that however great may be the slaughter that is made of a certain species of animal (bison, beaver, caribou, etc.), extinction does not threaten it: its existence does not depend on that of individual animals.

These customs and beliefs proceed directly from the mystical orientation of these minds, which is thus expressed through a characteristic essential to their experience. Or, if a less general formula is preferred, they illuminate the sense of the often quoted formula familiar to the primitive mentality: 'Everything has an invisible as well as a visible existence.' This invisible existence explains many points that otherwise would not be explained in the visible existence of things—points that, in their turn, provide evidence for this invisible existence and reinforce the belief that there is in it. Recall here the persistence of the mythical world, the supernatural simultaneously transcendental and immanent in nature: what precedes is an illustration of it.

February 9th, 1939.

PASSAGE TO PARTICIPATION

When a being or an event strikes the primitive man by its abnormal appearance, the affective category of the supernatural comes into action. At the same moment, the general conditions of experience change. The conditions of time and place, and the ordinary causal nexus are no longer applied: the supernatural force does not submit to them; on the contrary it is the supernatural force that disposes of them. It is the cause, but not after the fashion of secondary causes.

Likewise, when in a living thing, an animal for example, the primitive man's attention is fixed on its properties, on its invisible powers, it is looked at from the point of view of the mystical experience.

At the time it is not only the animal that he perceives *hic et nunc*, with its characteristics as given in ordinary experience, that occupies his thought: it is the animal in so far as it manifests these mystical powers, or, more exactly, it is these mystical powers in so far as they are manifest in the animal here present. But these powers do not belong to it in so far as it is this particular animal, this actually perceived individual being. They belong similarly to the other animals of the same species: here again, accordingly, one of the conditions of experience is modified, the experience being mystical. The distinction between the individual here present and the others similar to it is disregarded. What concerns the primitive man is the supernatural force common to all these individuals, and of which each is, by the same right, a visible realization (see *supra*).

Thus each of them is a bearer of this supernatural force by virtue of a participation in the mystical source of this force, which the primitive mentality feels rather than represents (owner, boss of the species, its genius, its spirit, etc.). Many participations are even given or implied in this mystical experience: participation between this force and each of the individual animals or the totality of these animals taken collectively, by virtue of which

P

this force is manifested through them. And if one of the animals is considered, the one whose participation releases the action of the affective category of the supernatural in the present experience, this perception only produces this effect, only provokes this emotion because, for it to be what the primitive man feels it to be, has required a participation between it and this power of the supernatural world.

It thus appears that participation is *inherent* in this sort of experience or 'thought' (if this is not forcing the sense of the word too much). What makes participation seem something incompatible with the customary norms of the intellect is that, unless we are careful, we take for granted that, in the primitive mentality, things are *given* first and afterwards participate with some supernatural power or other, etc.—without us being able to understand how this participation can occur, how a thing can be simultaneously itself and other than itself (*How Natives Think*— Bororo-parrot, etc.). In effect here is an impasse, and we have established an indefinite number of participations in vain, for participation still causes us a certain unease.

But if we cannot get out of this impasse, we can at least not get fouled up in it. How is that? Simply by not taking for granted that things are *given* first and that afterwards they enter into participations. In order that they shall be given, that they shall exist, it is already necessary to have participations. A participation is not only a mysterious and inexplicable fusion of things that lose and preserve their identity simultaneously. Participation enters into the very constitution of these things. Without participation, they would not be *given* in experience: they would not exist. This will become clearer through some examples the full meaning of which is illuminated by a remark of Leenhardt quoted above: the primitive mentality does not know what an individuality subsisting on its own is: individuals, human or others, only exist in so far as they participate in their group and with their ancestors. Participation is thus *immanent* in the individual. For it is to it that it owes being what it is. It is a *condition of its existence*, perhaps the most important, the most essential. One might say: for this mentality to exist is to participate in a mystical force, essence and reality.

It is enough to open *How Natives Think* or one of the following volumes, in particular the last two, to find abundant proof of what has just been said. Consider for example the Aranda: how he feels himself a member of his group, how he is more and more closely integrated into it, the group living through him and he through the group—then the group itself inseparable from the mythical ancestors, from the period before there was time, from the sacred sites and from what is implied there, etc. . . . The impossibility for the individual to separate within himself what would be properly him and what he participates in in order to exist: which we cannot understand because it concerns a thought which is not conceptual, nor is it intuitive, and we can do no better than characterize it as a direct apprehension, a feeling, an experience-belief.

February 10–11th, 1939.

UNRESOLVED DIFFICULTIES

What precedes ought to lead me to something definite concerning participation, but this is still not as matters stand. We have established only what concerns the conditions of time, place and the causal nexus when the primitive mentality finds itself in the presence of a mystical experience, or, better put, when an experience takes the mystical character, that is to say feels the supernatural in the natural—and what concerns the distinction of one and many in the same circumstances. That the affective category of the supernatural may be linked to this mental attitude is not in doubt: neither is the fact that this category may, at the same time, be linked to participation. But it remains to discover and to show of what these relations consist, to demonstrate how the same attitude, the same mental orientation 'understands', that it to say unites, produces jointly what I have called mystical experience, more or less clear feeling and representation of a supernatural or mythical world with its fluidity and other characteristics, the affective category of the supernatural and finally participation. The difficulty seems to be that there is no question there of objectively distinct realities, nor of finding middle terms in order to pass from one to the other, but rather of aspects of a single psychic activity and of complexes where it expresses it and is manifest, the part of the affective being there very great and even most often predominant, whence it follows that our philosophical and psychological terminology is cruelly inadequate, and continually risks falsifying the description. Finally it seems impossible that this description be satisfying if it is made solely from the point of view of psychology: it is absolutely necessary that it be treated at the same time from the point of view of sociology. For the mystical experience is inseparable from beliefs (Hallowell), and even the feeling and the representation of the supernatural (equals the mythical world) involve myths, social elements of the first rank.

Accordingly to re-examine successively each of these aspects by showing their solidarity with the others—and, before passing to participation, distinguish the different sorts of it, and also try to isolate what they have in common.

February 13th, 1939.

Index

Index

Force, immanent, 119; invisible, 24, 26, 91, 97, 102, 140; mystical, xviii, xx, 192; natural, 133; supernatural, 23–4, 26, 29, 42, 43, 51, 52, 53, 54, 59, 88, 132, 133, 134, 135, 140, 142, 181, 182, 184, 186, 187–8, 189, 191; transcendant; 119

France, 174

Frazer, 159

Freud, 80

Gabon, 172

Generality, 66, 90, 103; affective, 59–60; logical, 59–60

Generalization, 64, 66, 127, 169

Group. *See* Social Group

Grubb, 5–6, 7, 40, 74, 117

Guinea, xvii, 21, 40, 41

Hallowell, 90, 92, 123, 151, 194

History, xiii, xx, xxii, 56, 62, 63, 97, 98, 105, 124, 141, 149; mythical, 148; sacred, 64, 149; true, 12, 62, 147, 148, 149

Howitt, 79

How Natives Think, xiii, xiv, xvi, xix, xx, xxiii–xxiv, xxv, 18, 37, 38, 39, 48, 58, 60, 61, 62, 64, 65, 66, 67, 85, 87, 99, 100, 101, 104, 105, 120, 124, 126, 127, 135, 142, 143, 169, 171, 173, 174, 189, 192

Human being, 9, 50

Human group. *See* Social group

Human mentality. *See* Mentality, human

Human mind. *See* Mind, human

Human progress. *See* Evolution

Hume, 27, 97, 172

Hutton, 114

Idea, xv, 35; abstract, 10, 14, 70; general, 32, 34, 35, 36, 37, 66; generic, 33

Identity, 73, 76, 102, 106, 108, 166. *See also* Participation, equals community of essence

Image, 10, 34, 35, 36, 75, 106, 111; generic, 33, 34, 35, 36, 37

Imitation, 60, 108–9, 111, 112; *See also* Participation, equals imitation

Impossibility, logical, 7, 8, 12, 62; physical, 7, 8, 12, 62, 130, 140, 170, 173, 176

Impossible, the, 51–5, 57, 140, 193

Im Thurn, 135

Incompatibility, xv, 6, 7–11, 12, 41, 42, 43, 44, 45, 46, 49, 51, 53, 54, 58, 87, 96, 117, 125, 126, 130, 136, 137, 160; physical, 19, 121, 126, 130; primitive mentality indifferent to, 49, 50, 121, 137

Indians, 29, 40; North American, 36, 152, 163, 185

Individual, the, xxii, 4, 12, 13, 14, 17, 18, 20, 27, 28, 32, 35, 36, 50, 51, 59, 61, 64, 66, 67, 68, 69, 70, 71, 72, 75, 76, 77, 78, 79, 80, 81, 83, 84, 88, 89, 91, 92, 93, 95, 96, 97, 106, 107, 108, 109, 112, 113, 115–16, 123, 124, 153, 154, 155, 157, 160, 163, 190, 191, 192, 193; appurtenance as, 124. *See also* Participation, between individual and his appurtenances

Individuality, xxiii, 75, 77, 78, 96, 97, 114, 122, 124, 190, 192

Individuality-plurality, 96

Indonesia, 172

Induction, 10–11, 60

Initiation, 15, 66, 75, 94, 115, 137

Inquiry, mystical. *See* Divination

Irrational, the, 99

Isolation, 143

Junod, 73, 86, 174

Juxtapositions, xv, 58, 59, 60, 66, 85

Kanaka, 59, 79, 88, 97, 150, 151

Kant, xii, 27, 55, 56, 91

Kingsley, 96

Kipsigis, 185–6

Knowledge, theory of, 1, 27, 76–7